Ida Mett was born as Ida Mark[ ]
Smorgon in the Russian Empire (
antly Jewish, the small industrial
became an anarchist while studying medicine in Moscow. She was
soon arrested for 'anti-Soviet activities' and was expelled from the
country with her first husband, David Tennenbaum, in 1924.

In 1925, Ida was in Paris. Here she became involved with the
Group of Russian Anarchists Abroad, which included the great
fighter Nestor Makhno, his sometime collaborator Peter Arshinov,
and fellow anarcho-syndicalist Nicolas Lazarévitch, who she later
married. As well as editing the journal, *Dielo Truda* (Workers'
Cause), Mett was one of the co-authors of the Group's controversial
but influential '*Organisational Platform of the General Union of
Anarchists (Draft)*' – the Platform.

1931 found her celebrating May Day with anarchist heroes
Buenaventura Durruti and Francisco Ascaso in Barcelona. Present at
this meeting were also the veteran Russian anarchist Voline, Augustin
Souchy (author of *With the Peasants of Aragon*, available from this
publisher) and Camilo Berneri (murdered by the Communists during
the Barcelona May Events of 1937).

Back in Paris, Ida served as secretary of the local gas workers'
union, all the time writing and agitating, being arrested many times.
It was in this period that the booklet you are reading now was written.

After the Fall of France in 1940, Mett was briefly interned by the
Vichy regime in Rieucros camp, before the renegade Communist
Boris Souvarine successfully arranged her release. She spent the rest
of the war, with her husband and their ten year old son Marc, in La
Garde-Freinet, a quiet mountain village near the Côte d'Azur.

Returning to Paris, post-war Ida worked as a nurse in a sanat-
orium for Jewish children in Brunoy, and later as a translator. She
was never able to practice as a doctor because her qualifications were
not recognised by the authorities. During the events of May 1968, she
and her husband could be found on the streets of Paris discussing her
experiences with a new generation of radicals. She died on June 27th,
1973, aged 71.

The Kronstadt Uprising

Ida Mett

THEORY AND PRACTICE

'*La Commune de Cronstadt*'
First published 1938 by Éditions Spartacus, Paris

First English edition published 1967 as
'The Kronstadt Commune'
by Solidarity, London

Murray Bookchin introduction from 1971 Black Rose Books
(Montreal) edition.

This edition
2017 Theory and Practice

www.theoryandpractice.org.uk

Paperback ISBN: 978-0-9956609-4-6
Ebook ISBN: 978-0-9956609-5-3

Cover photo shows Kronstadt sailors of the Battleship Petropavlovsk in
Helsinki, 1917.
With thanks to Nick Heath for biographical information on Ida Mett.

Publishers Preface

If back in 1938, the events of Kronstadt were back in 'the days of the Egyptian Pharaohs', how much more irrelevant are they today? All the participants are long dead, shot down on the ice, purged by Stalin, or succumbed to old age. Why should we be bothered by what happened a hundred years ago? Because history is important. It gives us inspiration and example. It tells us what to expect.

And if the past is dead and gone, why is it that certain folk are always so keen to 'correct' the record? Because some of the most visible and persistent elements of present day so-called anti-capitalism still use the Russian Revolution as their model. The Soviet Union might be dead but its traditions weigh like a nightmare on the living.

Since the libertarian-socialist group *Solidarity* resurrected *The Kronstadt Commune* in the 1960s, there have been dozens of far more 'historically accurate' accounts. So why read Mett when you've got Avrich? Avrich, Getzler et al. are professional historians, their work coolly unbiased, meticulously researched, painstakingly presented. Mett's book is a polemic, a propaganda piece. Ida Mett had passion! Through her work, we share the outrage with her and her comrades, expelled, beaten, murdered by the 'Revolutionary Homeland' for revolutionary activities. And even after this extent of time, we should still be outraged. These were our comrades, our fellow workers, shot down to stop the incipient 'Third Revolution' in its tracks.

Unlike the professionals, Mett makes no excuses for the actions of the Bolsheviks in 1921. Neither peasant ignorance nor economic collapse but 'bureaucratisation' is to blame. And where, we might ask, does this come from? Straight from the practice and principles of the tankies, Trotskyists and Labourites! Amongst these, substitutionism – the party for the class – is not the exception but the rule. Bureaucrats, politicians, practical people, your 'leaders', will tell you they know better than you. This contempt for the people, who are capable only of 'trade union consciousness' turns us into followers, tools to be used in the streets or in the voting booth, with the aim of gaining power. And then it is a short step from doing things *for* the people, to doing things *to* them.

July, 2017

Introduction by Murray Bookchin

On March 1, 1921, the Kronstadt naval base on Kotlin Island, some twenty-five miles offshore from Petrograd adopted a fifteen-point program of political and economic demands – a program in open defiance of the Bolshevik Party's control of the Soviet state.

Almost immediately the Bolsheviks denounced the uprising as a 'White Guard plot,' ostensibly another in the series of counter-revolutionary conspiracies that had beleaguered the Soviet regime during the three preceding years of civil war. Less than three weeks later, on March 17, Kronstadt was subdued in a bloody assault by select Red Army units. The Kronstadt uprising, to all appearances, had been little more than a passing episode in the bitter history of the civil war.

We can now say, however, that the Kronstadt uprising marked the definitive end of the Russian Revolution itself. Indeed, the character and importance of the uprising were destined to become issues of acrimonious dispute within the international Left for years to come. Today, although an entirely new generation of revolutionaries has emerged – a generation almost totally uninformed of the events – the 'problem of Kronstadt' has lost none of its relevance and poignancy. For the Kronstadt uprising posed very far-reaching issues: the relationship between the so-called 'masses' and the parties which profess to speak in their name, and the nature of the social system in the modern Soviet Union. The Kronstadt uprising, in effect, remains as a lasting challenge to the Bolshevik concept of a party's historical function and the notion of the Soviet Union as a 'workers' or 'socialist' state.

The Kronstadt sailors were no ordinary military body. They were the famous 'Red Sailors' of 1905, 1917, and the civil war. By common consent (until the Bolsheviks began to revise history after the uprising) the Kronstadt sailors were regarded as the most reliable and politicised military elements of the newly established Soviet regime. Trotsky's feeble attempt in later years to debase their reputation by alluding to 'new' social strata (presumably 'peasants') that had replaced the 'original' Red Sailors (presumably 'workers') in Kronstadt during the civil war is beneath contempt. Whether 'peasants' or 'workers' – and both existed in varying numbers in the naval base – Kronstadt had long been the furnace of the revolution. Its living traditions and its close contact with 'Red Petrograd' served to anneal men of nearly all strata into revolutionaries.

In fact, Kronstadt had risen as a result of a strike movement in Petrograd, a near uprising by the Petrograd proletariat. It cannot be emphasized too strongly that the demands of the Kronstadt sailors were not formulated in the fastness of an isolated island in the Gulf of Finland: they were developed as a result of the close contact between the naval base and the restless Petrograd workers, whose demands the fifteen-point program essentially articulated. As Isaac Deutscher was obliged to acknowledge, the Bolshevik denunciations of the Kronstadt uprising as a 'White Guard plot' were simply groundless.

What were these demands? Ida Mett discusses them in detail in her book. A glance shows that the political demands centered around soviet democracy: new elections to the soviets, freedom of speech for Anarchists and Left Socialist parties, free trade unions and peasant organizations, the liberation of Anarchist and Socialist political prisoners. Economic and institutional demands focused on a loosening of the stringent trade restrictions imposed by the period of 'War Communism.' The demands of the Kronstadt sailors were the very minimum needed to rescue the revolution from bureaucratic decay and economic strangulation.

Ordinarily, there are two histories of revolutions. The first comprises the official history, a history which turns around the conflicts of parties, factions, and 'leaders.' The other, in the words of the Russian Anarchist, Voline, may be called the 'unknown revolution' – the rarely written accounts of independent, creative action by the revolutionary people. Marxian accounts, to a surprising extent, fall into the official form of historiography: popular aspects of the revolution are often distorted to accord with a predetermined social framework. The workers invariably have their assigned historical 'role'; the peasants a 'role' of their own; the intellectuals and Party, still other 'roles.' The vital, often decisive activity of so-called 'transitional classes,' such as workers of peasant origin or *déclassé* elements, are usually ignored. Owing to its simplistic mauling of social reality, this type of historiography leaves many crucial aspects of past and present-day revolutions completely unexplained.[1] Events acquire an academic form that is pieced together by programs, ideological clashes, and, of course, the ubiquitous 'leaders.'

In the Kronstadt uprising, the 'masses' had the effrontery to enter the historic stage again, as they did in February and

---

1   In Spain (1936), the Russian Revolution, the Paris Commune, the June uprising of the Parisian Workers in 1848, no less than in revolutionary upsurges today, the most dynamic elements were precisely members of these 'transitional classes.' *In the past*, they were mainly craftsmen, workers of peasant origin, and *déclassés, all of Marx's jibes to the contrary*. Today they consist of students, youth from nearly all classes, intellectuals, *déclassés*, and in the 'Third World', landless laborers and peasants.

October, four years earlier. In fact, the uprising marked the culmination and the end of the *popular* movement in the Russian Revolution – a movement the Bolshevik party basically mistrusted and shamelessly manipulated. The overthrow of Czarism in February, 1917 – a spontaneous revolution in which none of the Socialist parties and factions played a significant role – opened the way to a sweeping popular movement. Having shattered centuries-old institutions in a matter of days, the workers and peasants began *on their own initiative* to create new, entirely revolutionary social forms. Historical accounts of the revolution rarely tell us that in the cities, the most significant of these were not the soviets but rather the factory committees: bodies of workers established and controlled by workers' assemblies in the shops. In the villages, what has usually been designated as 'soviets' more closely corresponded to local committees of peasants, based on popular assemblies. In both cases, the committees were truly organic social bodies, wedded to direct, face-to-face democratic forms. By contrast, the regional soviets were essentially parliamentary bodies, structured as indirect or so-called 'representative' political hierarchies. These culminated in remote national congresses of soviets, controlled by a select executive committee.

The social history of the Revolution turned around the fate of the factory committees and village assemblies, not simply around conflicting armies and duels between the Bolsheviks and their political opponents. The factory committees demanded and, for a brief period, acquired full control over industrial operations. Lenin distrusted them completely after October. As early as January, 1919, only two months after 'decreeing' workers' control of the factories, the Bolshevik leader moved into open opposition to the committees. In Lenin's view, the revolution demanded 'precisely in the interests of socialism that the masses *unquestionably obey the single will* of the leaders of the labour process.' The committees were thereupon increasingly divested of any function in industrial operations their powers were transferred to the trade union and finally the powers of the unions delivered almost entirely to state appointed managers. Workers control was sharply denounced not only as 'inefficient', 'chaotic', and 'impractical' but as 'petit-bourgeois' and as 'anarcho-syndicalist deviation.'

In the countryside, Bolshevik policy was marked by a distrust of cooperatives and communes – and by expanding the use of forced requisitions of food. As I have indicated elsewhere, to Lenin the preferred, more 'socialist' form of agricultural enterprise was represented by the State Farm: literally, an agricultural factory in which the state owned the land and farming equipment, appointing managers who hire peasants on a wage basis.[2] By 1920, the Bolsheviks had isolated themselves completely from the working class and peasantry, a fact which Lenin openly acknowledged. Even the soviets had been hollowed into a political shell, divested of all content. Political life, public expression, and popular activity had come to a standstill; the Cheka, a secret police established under Dzerzhinsky, herded revolutionary oppositionists into jails and concentration camps. In increasing numbers, the more articulate spokesmen of independent soviet parties and groups were shot merely for the expression of dissident views. The policies formulated under the rubric of 'War Communism' created near famine conditions in the cities by blocking virtually all exchange between town and country and by imposing more demanding requisitions upon the peasantry. The

---

2   Cf. 'Listen Marxist!' *Anarchos* pamphlet, p.20

workers and peasants may have won the civil war, but this much is certain: they had lost the revolution.

Only in this political and economic context can we understand the strikes that swept Petrograd in February, 1921, and the uprising of the Kronstadt sailors. From Kronstadt the cry went up for a 'Third Revolution of the toilers,' not a counter-revolution to restore the past. By crushing the uprising, the Bolsheviks succeeded not only in blocking a third revolution, but in paving the way for the Stalinist regime. Later, history was to take its own savage revenge: many of the Bolsheviks who had played a role in putting down Kronstadt were to pay with their lives in the bloody purges of the thirties.

The main value of Ida Mett's work is the glimpse it gives us into the popular movement, a movement on which depends the outcome of all revolutionary upheavals. We are drawn away from the Party and soviet congresses, from the 'leaders' and the political factions, into the very soul of the revolutionary process. We gain a sense of the political insights evolved in the streets and barracks; we are brought into the molecular processes of the movement below; we establish contact with the remarkable spirit of popular improvisation, the enthusiasm and energy, that marks the revolutionary people in motion. For these reasons alone Mett's short work deserves the closest reading, for what is at stake in her account of Kronstadt is not the Russian Revolution alone, but the very concept of revolution itself.

The Bolshevik party did not 'make' the Russian Revolution; it *dominated* the revolution and thereby strangled it. It played no role whatever in February, 1917, when Czarism was overthrown; in October, eight months later, the party took power for itself, not on behalf of the soviets or the factory committees. Doubtless, conscious revolutionary organizations were necessary in 1917, or, at least, active groups of revolutionaries.

The real issue, however, was whether these revolutionary groups were capable of dissolving into the social forms created by the revolutionary people (be they factory committees or Soviets) or whether they turned into a separate power over these social forms, manipulating and finally destroying them. The Bolshevik party was constitutionally incapable of taking the first direction; its hierarchical, centralized structure, not to speak of the mentality of its leaders, had simply converted the party into a mirror image of the bourgeois state apparatus it claimed to overthrow.

During the debates that were to determine the fate of the factory committees, the Left Communist, Ossinsky warned his party: 'Socialism and socialist organization must be set up by the proletariat itself, or they will not be set up at all; something else will be set up – state capitalism.'

The warning, delivered in the early days of the revolution, was prophetic. It would be an utter absurdity to claim that a state apparatus which divests the workers of any control over society can be regarded as a 'workers state.' Actually, until 1917, all the major factions of the Russian Marxist movement believed that Russia was faced with a bourgeois revolution. Aside from organizations considerations, the disagreements between the Bolsheviks and Mensheviks centred primarily around the *political* role of the workers and peasants in the coming upheaval. By demanding a 'democratic dictatorship of the proletariat and peasantry,' the Bolsheviks were essentially calling for a politically dominant role by the oppressed. The Mensheviks, in turn, adhered essentially to the view that Russia required a democratic, parliamentary republic, governed by bourgeois parties. Neither of the two social-democratic factions were so naive as to believe that backward, agrarian Russia was prepared for a 'proletarian dictatorship,' much less for socialism.

The success of the February Revolution, however, caused Lenin to veer toward a 'proletarian dictatorship,' a position spelled out in the famous slogan: 'All power to the soviets!' Significant as this shift may have been, it was not rooted in any conviction on Lenin's part that Russia was suddenly prepared for a 'workers' state.' Quite to the contrary: Lenin viewed a 'proletarian revolution' in Russia primarily as a stimulus to socialist revolutions in the industrialised, war-torn countries of the West, notably Germany. To Lenin, the war had opened the prospect of revolutions abroad – revolutions that could be ignited by a 'proletarian revolution' in Russia. At no point did he deceive himself that a 'workers' state' or 'socialism' could be established within the confines of a predominantly peasant country.

The defeat of the Spartakus uprising in Berlin in January, 1919, left the Russian Revolution completely isolated. Despite the Marxian jargon of the new Soviet regime, despite its red flags and the obvious hostility of the traditional ruling classes at home and abroad, the fact remains that the revolution increasingly fell back to a bourgeois level, for it was inconceivable that an isolated, economically backward country, besieged by political enemies on every side, could advance beyond capitalist social relations.

But what type of capitalist social relations were created by the October Revolution? This was to remain a very knotty question. The revolution had eliminated the traditional Russian bourgeoisie and many of its political institutions. It had nationalized the land and all of industry, an unprecedented act in the modern history of Europe. Later, the Soviet regime was to institute 'planned production.' All of these changes in the early decades of the twentieth century were regarded as incompatible with capitalism, although Engels in

Anti-Dühring had toyed with the theoretical possibility that they could occur within a bourgeois framework.

The problems created by the October Revolution were further complicated by the terminology of the Bolsheviks themselves. Lenin had variously described the Soviet state as 'state capitalist', 'a workers' state,' and 'peasants' state with bureaucratic deformations,' to be followed by Trotsky's nonsensical description of the Stalinist dictatorship as 'degenerated workers' state.' Lenin also complicated the problem by crudely describing socialism as 'nothing but a state capitalist monopoly *made to benefit the whole people.*' Thus, in the early years of the Soviet regime, it was difficult not only to find parallels for state capitalism in any existing capitalist country, but to distinguish it from 'socialism.'

Today, after a half century of capitalist development we occupy a better vantage point. We can see that, except for the few months when the factory committees controlled industry, the Russian Revolution had by no means transcended a bourgeois social and economic framework. Commodity production and economic exploitation were destined to be as prevalent after the October Revolution as before. The workers and peasants were to be denied control over Soviet society as surely as they had been denied over Czarist society. We also know that nationalization of industry and planned production are perfectly compatible with bourgeois social relations. The historic trend of industrial capitalism has always been in the direction of the centralization of capital, the development of monopoly, the merging of industry with the state, economic planning, and finally the increasing power of a bureaucratic apparatus over economic and political life.

Ironically, Trotsky might have understood how this trend developed in Russia had he simply followed through his own concept of 'combined development' to its logical conclusion.

He saw (quite correctly) that Czarist Russia, latecomer in the European bourgeois development, necessarily acquired the most advanced industrial and class forms, instead of recapitulating the entire bourgeois development from its beginnings. He neglected to consider that Russia, torn by a tremendous internal upheaval which dispossessed the traditional bourgeois and land-owning classes, might have thereby run ahead of the capitalist development elsewhere in the world – certainly, after the workers and peasants were dispossessed of their control over the factories and land by the new bureaucracy. Hypnotized by the preposterous formula, 'nationalized property is antithetical to capitalism,' Trotsky failed to recognize that monopoly capitalism itself *tends to amalgamate with the state by its own inner dialectic, that involves the concentration of capital into fewer and fewer enterprises.* Lenin's analogy between 'socialism' and state capitalism thus became a terrifying reality under Stalin – a form of state capitalism that does *not* 'benefit the whole people.'

Fundamentally, the source of the confusion concerning the 'nature' of the social system in Russia – the famous 'Russian question' – lay in the incompleteness of the Marxian economic analysis. Writing in the mid-nineteenth century, Marx was familiar only with two phases of the capitalist development: mercantilism and 'laissez-faire' industrial capitalism. Although *Capital* brilliantly delineates the emergence of industrial from mercantile capitalism, the discussion ends precisely where it must begin for us a century later. We can see that the concentration of capital advances into still another phase: the *statification* of capital. The 'free market' passes into a monopolistic and finally a state-manipulated market. The 'anarchy of production' (to use Engels' phrase) passes into the managed, 'planned' economy, a system of planning designed not only to avert economic crises but to promote capital accumulation. Capitalism follows through its dialectic in almost classical Hegelian terms: from the state-controlled economy initiated by mercantilism into the 'free market' established by industrial capitalism and back again to neo-mercantilist forms, but on the new level created by technological and industrial growth. Marx could not be expected to follow this dialectic to its conclusion a century ago; for us to ignore it, a century later, would be theoretical myopia of the worst possible kind.

The development toward state capitalism appears as a *tendency* in the West primarily because early economic and political forms still exercise a powerful influence upon social institutions. Although waning rapidly, the notions of the 'free market' and the 'sovereign individual' continue to pervade economic relations in Europe and America. In Russia and many areas of the 'Third World,' however, state capitalism assumes a complete form because revolutions rupture the present from the past, leading to the destruction of the older ruling classes and institutions. 'Socialism' in its accepted Marxian form tends to become ideology in the narrowest sense of the term precisely because, as Lenin observed, so much of Marxian socialism can be identified with state capitalism. Marx's acceptance of the state – the 'proletarian dictatorship,' the 'socialist state' – becomes the vehicle for transmuting the great socialist vision into a totally reactionary spectacle: the red flags which drape the coffin of the popular revolution.

What might have happened had Kronstadt succeeded? We certainly would have been spared a Stalinist development, a development which turned the entire world Communist movement into an instrument of international counter-revolution. In the end, it was not only Russia that suffered brutally, but humanity as a whole. The legacy left to us by Bolshevism in the forms of Stalinism, Trotskyism, and Maoism, has burdened revolutionary thought and praxis as much as the betrayals of the reformist wings of the socialist movement.

A victory by the Kronstadt sailors might have also opened a new perspective for Russia – a hybrid social development combining workers' control of factories with an open market in agricultural goods, based on a small-scale peasant economy and voluntary agrarian communes. Certainly, such a society in backward agrarian Russia could not have stabilized itself for very long without outside aid; but aid might have been forth-coming had the revolutionary movement of Europe and Asia developed freely, without interference from the Third Interna-tional. Stalinism foreclosed this possibility completely. By the late twenties, virtually all sections of the Communist Interna-tional had become instruments of Stalinist policy, to be marketed in exchange for diplomatic and military alliances with the capitalist powers.

The suppression of Kronstadt in March 1921, was an act of outright counter-revolution, the throttling of the popular movement at a time when Lenin, Trotsky, and other outstanding Bolsheviks stood at the helm of the Soviet regime. To speak as Trotsky does, of the 'continuity' of the Russian Revolution into the thirties, to describe the bureaucracy as the guardian of the victories of October, to call Stalinism merely a 'Thermidorean' reaction – all of this is sheer nonsense. There is neither continuity nor Thermidor; merely the window dressing for a vision that was throttled in 1921 and even earlier. Stalin's accession to power merely underscored a counter-revolution that had begun earlier. Long before 1927, when the Trotskyist opposition was expelled, all the social gains had been erased so far as the Russian people were concerned. Hence the indifference of the workers and peasants to the anti-Stalinist opposition movements within the Communist Party.

All the conditions for Stalinism were prepared by the defeat of the Kronstadt sailors and Petrograd strikers. We may choose to lament these popular movements, to honour the heroism of the victims, to inscribe their efforts in the annals of the revolution. But above all the Kronstadt revolt and the strike movement in Petrograd must be understood – as we would understand the lessons of all the great revolutions – if we are to grasp the content of the revolutionary process itself.

1971.

Preface to Solidarity Edition

The fiftieth anniversary of the Russian Revolution will be assessed, analysed, celebrated or bemoaned in a variety of ways.

To the peddlers of religious mysticism and to the advocates of 'freedom of enterprise', Svetlana Stalin's sensational (and well-timed) defection will 'prove' the resilience of their respective doctrines, now shown as capable of sprouting on what at first sight would appear rather barren soil.

To incorrigible liberals, the recent, cautious reintroduction of the profit motive into certain sectors of the Russian economy will 'prove' that laissez-faire economics is synonymous with human nature and that a rationally planned economy was always a pious pipe-dream.

To those 'lefts' (like the late Isaac Deutscher) who saw in Russia's industrialization an automatic guarantee of more liberal attitudes in days to come, the imprisonment of Daniel and Sinyavsky for thought-crime (and the current persecution of those who stood up for them) will have come as a resounding slap in the face.

To the 'Marxist-Leninists' of China (and Albania), Russia's rapprochement with the USA, her passivity in the recent Middle East crisis, her signing of the Test Ban Treaty and her reactionary influence on revolutionary developments in the colonial countries will all bear testimony to her headlong slither into the swamp of revisionism, following the Great

Stalin's death. (Stalin, it will be remembered, was the architect of such revolutionary, non-revisionist, measures as the elimination of the Old Bolsheviks, the Moscow Trials, the Popular Front, the Nazi-Soviet Pact, the Teheran and Yalta Agreements and the dynamic struggles of the French and Italian Communist Parties in the immediate post-war years, struggles which led to their direct seizure of power in their respective countries.)

To the Yugoslavs, reintegrated at last after their adolescent wandering from the fold, the re-emergence of 'sanity' in Moscow will be seen as corroboration of their worst suspicions. The 1948 'troubles' were clearly all due to the machinations of the wicked Beria. Mihajlo Mihajlov now succeeds Djilas behind the bars of a people's prison... just to remind political heretics that, in Yugoslavia too, 'proletarian democracy' is confined to those who refrain from asking awkward questions.

To the Trotskyists of all ilk – at least to those still capable of thinking for themselves – the mere fact of the fiftieth anniversary celebrations should be food for thought. What do words mean? How 'transitional' can a transitional society be? Aren't four decades of 'Bonapartism' in danger of making the word a trifle meaningless? Like the unflinching Christians carrying their cross, will unflinching Trotskyists go on carrying their question mark (concerning the future evolution of Russian society) for the rest of their earthly existence? For how much longer will they go on gargling with the old slogans of 'capitalist restoration or advance towards socialism' proposed by their mentor in his *Revolution Betrayed* ... thirty years ago! Surely only the blind can now fail to see that Russia is a class society of a new type, and has been for several decades.

Those who have shed these mystifications – or who have never been blinded by them – will see things differently. They will sense that there can be no vestige of socialism in a society whose rulers can physically annihilate the Hungarian Workers' Councils, denounce equalitarianism and workers' management of production as 'petty-bourgeois' or 'anarcho-syndicalist' deviations, and accept the cold-blooded murder of a whole generation of revolutionaries as mere 'violations of socialist legality', to be rectified – oh so gingerly and tactfully – by the technique of 'selective posthumous rehabilitation'. It will be obvious to them that something went seriously wrong with the Russian Revolution. *What was it? And when did the 'degeneration' start?*

Here again the answers differ. For some the 'excesses' or 'mistakes' are attributable to a spiteful paranoia slowly sneaking up on the senescent Stalin. This interpretation (apart from tacitly accepting the very 'cult of the individual' which its advocates would claim to decry) fails, however, to account for the repressions of revolutionaries and the conciliations with imperialism perpetrated at a much earlier period. For others the 'degeneration' set in with the final defeat of the Left Opposition as an organized force (1927), or with Lenin's death (1924), or with the abolition of factions at the tenth Party Congress (1921). For the Bordigists the proclamation of the New Economic Policy (1921) irrevocably stamped Russia as 'state capitalist'. Others, rightly rejecting this preoccupation with the minutiae of revolutionary chronometry, stress more general factors, albeit in our opinion some of the less important ones.

Our purpose in publishing this text about the Kronstadt events of 1921 is not to draw up an alternative timetable. Nor are we looking for political ancestors. The construction of an orthodox apostolic succession is the least of our preoccupations. (In a constantly changing world it would only testify to our theoretical sterility.) Our occupation is simply to document some of the real – but less well-known – struggles that took place against the growing bureaucracy during the early post-revolutionary years, at a time when most of the later critics of the bureaucracy were part and parcel of the apparatus itself.

The fiftieth anniversary of the Russian Revolution presents us with the absurd sight of a Russian ruling class (which every day resembles more its Western counterpart) solemnly celebrating the revolution which overthrew bourgeois power and allowed the masses, for a brief moment, to envisage a totally new kind of social order.

What made this tragic paradox possible? What shattered this vision? How did the Revolution degenerate?

Many explanations are offered. The history of how the Russian working class was dispossessed is not, however, a matter for an esoteric discussion among political cliques, who compensate for their own irrelevance by mental journeys into the enchanted world of the revolutionary past. An understanding of what took place is essential for every serious socialist. It is not mere archivism.

No viable ruling class rules by force alone. To rule it must succeed in getting its own vision of reality accepted by society at large. The concepts by which it attempts to legitimize its rule must be projected into the past. Socialists have correctly recognized that the history taught in bourgeois schools reveals a particular, distorted, vision of the world. It is a measure of the weakness of the revolutionary movement that *socialist* history remains for the most part unwritten.

What passes as socialist history is often only a mirror image of bourgeois historiography, a percolation into the ranks of the working class movement of typically bourgeois methods of thinking. In the world of this type of 'historian' leaders of genius replace the kings and queens of the bourgeois world. Famous congresses, splits or controversies, the rise and fall of political parties or unions, the emergence or degeneration of this or that leadership replace the internecine battles of the rulers of the past. The masses never appear independently on the historical stage, making their own history. At best they only 'supply the steam', enabling others to drive the loco-motive, as Stalin so delicately put it.

'Most of the time, 'official' historians don't have eyes to see or ears to hear the acts and words which express the workers' spontaneous activity ... They lack the categories of thought – one might even say the brain cells – necessary to understand or even to perceive this activity as it really is. To them an activity that has no leader or programme, no institutions and no statutes, can only be described as 'troubles' or 'disorders'. The spontaneous activity of the masses belongs by definition to what history suppresses.'[1]

This tendency to identify working class history with the history of its organizations, institutions and leaders is not only inadequate – it reflects a typically bourgeois vision of mankind, divided in almost preordained manner between *the few* who will manage and decide, and the *many*, the malleable mass, incapable of acting consciously on its own behalf, and forever destined to remain the object (and never the subject) of history. Most histories of the degeneration of the Russian Revolution rarely amount to more than this.

The Stalinist bureaucracy was unique in that it presented a view of history based on outright lies rather than on the more usual mixture of subtle distortion and self-mystification. But Khrushchev's revelations and subsequent developments in

---

1   Paul Cardan, *From Bolshevism to the Bureaucracy* (Solidarity Pamphlet 24).

Russia have caused official Russian versions of events (in all their variants) to be questioned even by members of the Communist Party. Even the graduates of what Trotsky called 'the Stalin school of falsification' are now beginning to reject the lies of the Stalinist era. Our task is to take the process of demystification a little further.

Of all the interpretations of the degeneration of the Russian Revolution that of Issac Deutscher is the most widely accepted on the Left. It echoes most of the assumptions of the Trotsky-ists. Although an improvement on the Stalinist versions, it is hardly sufficient. The degeneration is seen as due to strictly conjunctural factors (the isolation of the revolution in a back-ward country, the devastation caused by the Civil War, the overwhelming weight of the peasantry, etc.). These factors are undoubtedly very important. But the growth of the bureau-cracy is more than just an accident in history. It is a worldwide phenomenon, intimately linked to a certain stage in the devel-opment of working class consciousness. It is the terrible price paid by the working class for its delay in recognizing that the true and final emancipation of the working class can only be achieved by the working class itself, and cannot be entrusted to others, allegedly acting on its behalf. If 'socialism is Man's total and positive self-consciousness' (Marx, 1844), the experience (and rejection) of the bureaucracy is a step on that road.

The Trotskyists deny that early oppositions to the devel-oping bureaucracy had any revolutionary content. On the contrary they denounce the Workers' Opposition and the Kronstadt rebels as basically counter-revolutionary. Real opposition, for them, starts with the proclamation – within the Party – of the Left Opposition of 1923. But anyone in the least familiar with the period will know that by 1923 the working class had already sustained a decisive defeat. It had lost power in production to a group of managers appointed from above.

It had also lost power in the Soviets, which were now only ghosts of their former selves, only a rubber stamp for the emerging bureaucracy. The Left Opposition fought within the confines of the Party, which was itself already highly bureaucratized. No substantial number of workers rallied to its cause. Their will to struggle had been sapped by the long struggle of the preceding years.

Opposition to the anti-working-class measures being taken by the Bolshevik leadership in the years immediately following the revolution took many forms and expressed itself through many different channels and at many different levels. It expressed itself *within* the Party itself, through a number of oppositional tendencies of which the Workers' Opposition (Kollontai, Lutovinov, Shlyapnikov) is the best known.[2] Outside the Party the revolutionary opposition found heterogenous expression, in the life of a number, often illegal groups (some anarchist, some anarcho-syndicalist, some still professing their basis faith in Marxism).[3] It also found expression in spontaneous, often 'unorganized' class activity, such as the big Leningrad strikes of 1921 and the Kronstadt uprising. It found expression in the increasing resistance of the workers to Bolshevik industrial policy (and in particular to Trotsky's attempts to militarize the trade unions). It also found expression in proletarian opposition to Bolshevik attempts to evict all other tendencies from the Soviets, thus effectively gagging all those seeking to re-orient socialist construction along entirely different lines.

---

2 For information concerning their programme see *The Workers' Opposition* by Alexandra Kollontai. This was first published in English in Sylvia Pankhurst's *Workers' Deadnought* in 1921 and republished in 1961 as Solidarity Pamphlet 8.

3 The history of such groups as the *Workers' Truth* group or the *Workers' Struggle* group still remains to be written.

At an early stage several tendencies had struggled against the bureaucratic degeneration of the Revolution. By posthumously excluding them from the ranks of the revolutionary, Trotskyists, Leninists and others commit a double injustice. Firstly they excommunicate all those who foresaw and struggled against the nascent bureaucracy *prior to 1923*, thereby turning a deaf ear to some of the most pertinent and valid criticisms ever voiced against the bureaucracy. Secondly they weaken their own case, for if the demands for freely elected Soviets, for freedom of expression (proletarian democracy) and for workers' management of production were wrong in 1921, why did they become partially correct in 1923? Why are they correct now? If in 1921 Lenin and Trotsky represented the 'real interests' of the workers (against the actual workers), why couldn't Stalin? Why couldn't Kadar in Hungary in 1956? The Trotskyist school of hagiography has helped to obscure the real lessons of the struggle against the bureaucracy.

When one seriously studies the crucial years after 1917, when the fate of the Russian Revolution was still in the melting pot, one is driven again and again to the tragic events of the Kronstadt uprising of March 1921. These events epitomize, in a bloody and dramatic manner, the struggle between two concepts of the Revolution, two revolutionary methods, two types of revolutionary ethos. Who decides what is or is not in the long term interests of the working class? What methods are permissible in settling differences between revolutionaries? And what methods are double-edged and only capable in the long run of harming the Revolution itself?

There is remarkably little of a detailed nature available in English about the Kronstadt events. The Stalinist histories, revised and re-edited according to the fluctuating fortunes of Party functionaries, are not worth the paper they are written on. They are an insult to the intelligence of their readers, deemed incapable of comparing the same facts described in earlier and later editions of the same book.

Trotsky's writings about Kronstadt are few and more concerned at retrospective justification and at scoring debating points against the Anarchists[4] than at seriously analysing this particular episode of the Russian Revolution. Trotsky and the Trotskyists are particularly keen to perpetuate the myth that they were the first and only coherent anti-bureaucratic tendency. All their writings seek to hide how far the bureaucratization of both Party and Soviets had already gone by 1921 – i.e. how far it had gone during the period when Lenin and Trotsky were in full and undisputed control. The task for serious revolutionaries today is to see the link between Trotsky's attitudes and pronouncements during and before the 'great trade union debate' of 1920-21 and the healthy hostility to Trotskyism of the most advanced and revolutionary layers of the industrial working class. This hostility was to manifest itself – arms in hand – during the Kronstadt uprising. It was to manifest itself again two or three years later – this time by folded arms – when these advanced layers failed to rally to Trotsky's support, when he at last chose to challenge Stalin, within the limited confines of a Party machine, towards whose bureaucratization he had signally contributed.[5]

---

4   An easy enough task after 1936, when some well-known anarchist 'leaders' (sic!) entered the Popular Front government in Catalonia at the beginning of the Spanish Civil War – and were allowed to remain there by the anarchist rank and file. This action – in an area where the anarchists had a mass basis in the labour movement – irrevocably damned them, just as the development of the Russian Revolution had irrevocably damned the Mensheviks, as incapable of standing up to the test of events.

5   Three statements from Trotsky's *Terrorism and Communism* (Ann Arbor: University of Michigan Press, 1961), first published in June 1920, will illustrate the point:

    'The creation of a socialist society means the organization of the work-

Deutscher in *The Prophet Armed* vividly depicts the background of Russia during the years of Civil War, the suffering, the economic dislocation, the sheer physical exhaustion of the population. But the picture is one-sided, its purpose to stress that the 'iron will of the Bolsheviks' was the only element of order, stability and continuity in a society that was hovering on the brink of total collapse. He pays scant attention to the attempts made by groups of workers and revolutionaries – both within the Party and outside its ranks – to attempt social reconstruction on an entirely different basis, from below.[6] He does not discuss the sustained opposition and hostility of the Bolsheviks to workers' management of production[7] or in fact

---

ers on new foundations, their adaptation to those foundations and their labour re-education, with the one unchanging end of the increase in the productivity of labour ...' (p. 146).

'I consider that if the Civil War had not plundered our economic organs of all that was strongest, most independent, most endowed with initiative, we should undoubtedly have entered the path of one-man management in the sphere of economic administration much sooner and much less painfully' (pp. 162-163).

'We have been more than once accused of having substituted for the dictatorship of the Soviets the dictatorship of our own Party ... In the substitution of the power of the Party for the power of the working class there is nothing accidental, and in reality there is no substitution at all. The Communists express the fundamental interests of the working class ...' (p. 109).

So much for the 'anti-bureaucratic' antecedents of Trotskyism. It is interesting that the book was highly praised by Lenin. Lenin only took issue with Trotsky on the trade union question at the Central Committee meeting of November 8 and 9, 1920. Throughout most of 1920 Lenin had endorsed all Trotsky's bureaucratic decrees in relation to the unions.

6 For an interesting account of the growth of the Factory Committees Movement – and of the opposition to them of the Bolsheviks at the First Ail-Russian Trade Union Convention (January 1918), see Maximov's *The Guillotine at Work* (Chicago, 1940).

7 At the Ninth Party Congress (March 1920) Lenin introduced a resolution to the effect that the task of the unions was to explain the need for a 'maximum curtailment of administrative collegia and the gradual introduction

to any large-scale endeavour which escaped their domination or control. Of the Kronstadt events themselves, of the Bolshevik calumnies against Kronstadt and of the frenzied repression that followed the events of March 1921, Deutscher says next to nothing, except that the Bolshevik accusations against the Kronstadt rebels were 'groundless'. Deutscher totally fails to see the direct relation between the methods used by Lenin and Trotsky in 1921 and those other methods, perfected by Stalin and later used against the Old Bolsheviks themselves during the notorious Moscow trials of 1936, 1937 and 1938.

In Victor Serge's *Memoirs of a Revolutionary* there is a chapter devoted to Kronstadt.[8] Serge's writings are particularly interesting in that he was in Leningrad in 1921 and supported what the Bolsheviks were doing, albeit reluctantly. He did not however resort to the slanders and misrepresentations of other leading Party members. His comments throw light on the almost schizophrenic frame of mind of the rank and file of the Party at that time. For different reasons neither the Trotskyists nor the anarchists have forgiven Serge his attempts to recon-cile what was best in their respective doctrines: the concern with reality and the concern with principle.

Easily available and worthwhile *anarchist* writings on the subject (in English) are virtually non-existent, despite the fact that many anarchists consider this area relevant to their ideas. Emma Goldman's *Living My Life* and Berkman's *The Bolshevik Myth* contain some vivid but highly subjective pages about the

---

of individual management in units directly engaged in production' (Robert V. Daniels, *The Conscience of the Revolution* (Cambridge, Mass., 1960), p. 124).

8   Serge's writings on this matter were first brought to the attention of read-ers in the UK in 1961 (Solidarity, I, 7). This text was later reprinted as a pamphlet.

Kronstadt rebellion. *The Kronstadt Revolt* by Anton Ciliga (produced as a pamphlet in 1942) is an excellent short account which squarely faces up to some of the fundamental issues. It has been unavailable for years. Voline's account, on the other hand, is too simplistic. Complex phenomena like the Kronstadt revolt cannot be meaningfully interpreted by loaded generalizations like 'as Marxists, authoritarians and statists, the Bolsheviks could not permit any freedom or independent action of the masses'. (Many have argued that there are strong Blanquist and even Bakuninist strands in Bolshevism, and that it is precisely these departures from Marxism that are at the root of Bolshevism's 'elitist' ideology and practice.) Voline even reproaches the Kronstadt rebels with 'speaking of power (the power of the Soviets) instead of getting rid of the word and of the idea altogether ...' The practical struggle however was not against 'words' or even 'ideas'. It was a physical struggle against their concrete incarnation in history (in the form of bourgeois institutions). It is a symptom of anarchist muddle-headedness on this score that they can both reproach the Bolsheviks with dissolving the Constituent Assembly[9] ... and the Kronstadt rebels for proclaiming that they stood for soviet power! The 'Soviet anarchists' clearly perceived what was at stake – even if many of their successors fail to. They fought to defend the deepest conquest of October – soviet power – against *all* its usurpers, including the Bolsheviks.

Our own contribution to the fiftieth anniversary celebrations will not consist in the usual panegyrics to the achievements of Russian rocketry. Nor will we chant paeans to Russian pig-iron statistics. Industrial expansion may be the prerequisite for a fuller, better life for all but is in no way synonymous with such a life, unless *all* social relations have

---

9 See Nicolas Walter's article in *Freedom* (October 28, 1967) entitled 'October 1917: No Revolution at All'.

been revolutionized. We are more concerned at the social costs of Russian achievements.

Some perceived what these costs would be at a very early stage. We are interested in bringing their prophetic warnings to a far wider audience. The final massacre at Kronstadt took place on March 18, 1921, exactly fifty years after the slaughter of the Communards by Thiers and Calliffet. The facts about the Commune are well known. But fifty years after the Russian Revolution we still have to seek basic information about Kron-stadt. The facts are not easy to obtain. They lie buried under the mountains of calumny and distortion heaped on them by Stalinists and Trotskyists alike.

The publication of this pamphlet in English, at this partic-ular time, is part of this endeavour. Ida Mett's book *La Commune de Cronstadt* was first published in 1938. It was republished in France ten years later but has been unobtain-able for several years. In 1962 and 1963 certain parts of it were translated into English and appeared in *Solidarity* (II, 6 to 11). We now have pleasure in bringing to English-speaking readers a slightly abridged version of the book as a whole, which contains material hitherto unavailable in Britain.[10]

Apart from various texts published in Kronstadt itself in March 1921, Ida Mett's book contains Petrichenko's open letter of 1926, addressed to the British Communist Party. Petrichenko was the President of the Kronstadt Provisional Revolutionary Committee. His letter refers to discussions in the Political Bureau of the CPGB on the subject of Kronstadt, discussions which seem to have accepted that there was no extraneous intervention during the uprising. (Members of the

---

10 Pages 9 – 21, dealing with the role of the Navy in the Russian revolution-ary movement have been omitted. Although they contain interesting and important material, which we hope will be translated in due course, they are not essential to the main argument.

CP and others might seek further enlightenment on the matter from King Street, whose archives on the matter should make interesting reading.)

Ida Mett writes from an anarchist viewpoint. Her writings however represent what is best in the revolutionary tradition of 'class struggle' anarchism. She thinks in terms of a collective, proletarian solution to the problems of capitalism. The rejection of the class struggle, the anti-intellectualism, the preoccupation with transcendental morality and with personal salvation that characterize so many of the anarchists of today should not for a minute detract 'Marxists' from paying serious attention to what she writes. We do not necessarily endorse all her judgments and have – in footnotes – corrected one or two minor factual inaccuracies in her text. Some of her generalizations seem to us too sweeping and some of her analyses of the bureaucratic phenomenon too simple to be of real use. But as a chronicle of what took place before, during and after Kronstadt, her account remains unsurpassed.

Her text throws interesting light on the attitude to the Kronstadt uprising shown at the time by various Russian political tendencies (anarchists, Mensheviks, Left and Right SRs, Bolsheviks, etc.). Some whose approach to politics is superficial in the extreme (and for whom a smear or a slogan is a substitute for real understanding) will point accusingly to some of this testimony, to some of these resolutions and manifestos as evidence irrevocably damning the Kronstadt rebels. 'Look', they will say, 'what the Mensheviks and Right SR's were saying. Look at how they were calling for a return to the Constituent Assembly, and at the same time proclaiming their solidarity with Kronstadt. Isn't this proof positive that Kronstadt was a counter-revolutionary upheaval? You yourselves admit that rogues like Victor Chernov, President elect of the

Constituent Assembly, offered to help the Kronstadters? What further evidence is needed?'

We are not afraid of presenting *all* the facts to our readers. Let them judge for themselves. It is our firm conviction that most Trotskyists and Leninists are – and are kept – as ignorant of this period of Russian history as Stalinists are of the period of the Moscow Trials. At best they vaguely sense the presence of skeletons in the cupboard. At worst they vaguely parrot what their leaders tell them, intellectually too lazy or politically too well-conditioned to probe for themselves. Real revolutions are never 'pure'. They unleash the deepest passions of men. People actively participate or are dragged into the vortex of such movements for a variety of often contradictory reasons. Consciousness and false consciousness are inextricably mixed. A river in full flood inevitably carries a certain amount of rubbish. A revolution in full flood carries a number of political corpses – and may even momentarily give them a semblance of life.

During the Hungarian Revolution of 1956 many were the messages of verbal or moral support for the rebels, emanating from the West, piously preaching the virtues of bourgeois democracy or of free enterprise. The objectives of those who spoke in these terms were anything but the institution of a classless society. But their support for the rebels remained purely verbal, particularly when it became clear to them what the real objectives of the revolution were: a fundamental democratization of Hungarian institutions *without* a reversion to private ownership of the means of production.

The backbone of the Hungarian revolution was the network of workers' councils. Their main demands were for workers' management of production and for a government based on the councils. These facts justified the support of revolutionaries throughout the world. Despite the Mindszentys. Despite the

Smallholders and Social-Democrats – or their shadows – now trying to jump on to the revolutionary bandwagon. The class criterion is the decisive one.

Similar considerations apply to the Kronstadt rebellion. Its core was the revolutionary sailors. Its main objectives were ones with which no real revolutionary could disagree. That others sought to take advantage of the situation is inevitable – and irrelevant. It is a question of who is calling the tune.

Attitudes to the Kronstadt events, expressed nearly fifty years after the event often provide deep insight into the political thinking of contemporary revolutionaries. They may in fact provide a deeper insight into their conscious or unconscious aims than many a learned discussion about economics, or philosophy, or about other episodes of revolutionary history.

It is a question of one's basic attitude as to what socialism is all about. What are epitomized in the Kronstadt events are some of the most difficult problems of revolutionary strategy and revolutionary ethics: the problems of ends and means, of the relations between Party and masses, in fact of whether a Party is necessary at all.

Can the working class by itself only develop a 'trade union consciousness'.[11] Should it even be allowed, at all times, to go that far?[12]

Or can the working class develop a deeper consciousness and understanding of its interests than can any organization allegedly acting on its behalf? When the Stalinists or Trotsky-

---

11 Lenin proclaimed so explicitly in his *What Is To Be Done?* (1902).

12 In a statement to the tenth Party Congress (1921) Lenin refers to a mere discussion on the trade unions as an 'absolutely impermissible luxury' which 'we' should not have permitted. These remarks speak unwitting volumes on the subject (and incidentally deal decisively with those who seek desperately for an 'evolution' in their Lenin).

ists speak of Kronstadt as 'an essential action against the class enemy', when more 'sophisticated' revolutionaries refer to it as a 'tragic necessity', one is entitled to pause for a moment. One is entitled to ask how seriously they accept Marx's dictum that 'the emancipation of the working class is the task of the working class itself'. Do they take this seriously or do they pay mere lip-service to the words? Do they identify socialism with the autonomy (organizational and ideological) of the working class? Or do they see themselves, with their wisdom as to the 'historical interests' of others, and with their judgments as to what should be 'permitted', as the leadership around which the future elite will crystallize and develop? One is entitled not only to ask... but also to suggest the answer!

November, 1967

Introduction to the French Edition

The time seems ripe for us to seek a better understanding of Kronstadt, although no new facts have emerged since 1921. The archives of the Russian Government and of the Red Army remain closed to any kind of objective analysis. However statements in some official publications seem to reflect some of these events, albeit in a distorted light. But what was known at the time was already sufficient to allow one to grasp the political significance of this symptomatic and crucial episode of the Russian Revolution.

Working class militants in the West had absolute confidence in the Bolshevik Government. This government had just headed an immense effort of the working class in its struggle against feudal and bourgeois reaction. In the eyes of these workers it incarnated the Revolution itself.

People could just not believe that this same government could have cruelly put down a revolutionary insurrection. That is why it was easy for the Bolsheviks to label the (Kronstadt) movement as a reactionary one and to denounce it as organized and supported by the Russian and European bourgeoisies.

'An insurrection of White generals, with ex-general Kazlovski at its head' proclaimed the papers at the time. Meanwhile the Kronstadt sailors were broadcasting the following appeal to the whole world:

'Comrade workers, red soldiers and sailors. We are for the power of the Soviets and not that of the parties. We are for free representation of all who toil. Comrades, you are being misled. At Kronstadt all power is in the hands of revolutionary sailors, of red soldiers and of workers. It is not in the hands of White Guards, allegedly headed by a general Kozlovski, as Moscow Radio tells you.'

Such were the conflicting interpretations of the Kronstadt sailors and of the Kremlin Government. As we wish to serve the vital interests of the working class by an objective analysis of historical events, we propose to examine these contradictory theses, in the light of facts and documents, and of the events that almost immediately followed the crushing of Kronstadt.

'The workers of the world will judge us' said the Kronstadters in their broadcast.

'The blood of the innocents will fall on the heads of those who have become drunk with power.' Was it a prophecy?

Here is a list of prominent communists having played an active part in the suppression of the insurrection. Readers will see their fate:

ZINOVIEV, omnipotent dictator of Petrograd. Inspired the implacable struggle against both strikers and sailors. *SHOT.*

TROTSKY, Peoples Commissar for War and for the Navy. *ASSASSINATED* by a Stalinist agent in Mexico.

LASHEVICH, member of the Revolutionary War Committee, member of Defence Committee organized to fight against the Petrograd strikers. Committed *SUICIDE.*

DYBENKO, veteran sailor. Before October, one of the organizers of the Central Committee of the Baltic Fleet, Played a particularly active role in the military crushing of Kronstadt. In 1938 still a garrison commander in the Petrograd region. *SHOT*.

KUZMIN, commissar to the Baltic Fleet. Fate unknown. *NEVER SPOKEN OF AGAIN*.

KALININ, remained in nominal power as 'President'. Died a *NATURAL DEATH*.

TUKHACHEVSKY, Elaborated the plan and led the assault on Kronstadt. *SHOT*.

PUTNA, decorated for his participation in the military suppression of Kronstadt, later military attaché in London. *SHOT*.

Delegates at the 10th Party Congress, who came to fight against Kronstadt:

PYATOKOV: *SHOT*

RUKHIMOVICH: *SHOT*

BUBNOV: *DEPOSED. DISAPPEARED.*

ZATONSKY: *DEPOSED. DISAPPEARED.*

VOROSHILOV: *STILL PLAYED A ROLE DURING THE 1941-45 WAR.* (Later President of Praesidium.)

Paris, October 1948.

The Kronstadt Events

'A new White plot ... expected and undoubtedly prepared by the French counter-revolution.' *Pravda*, March 3, 1921.

'White generals, you all know it, played a great part in this. This is fully proved.' Lenin, report delivered to the 10th Congress of the R.C.P.(B), March 8, 1921, *Selected Works*, vol. IX, p.98.

'The Bolsheviks denounced the men of Kronstadt as counter-revolutionary mutineers, led by a White general. The denunciation appears to have been groundless' Isaac Deutcher, *The Prophet Armed*, (Oxford University Press, 1954) p.511

'No pretence was made that the Kronstadt mutineers were White Guards.' Brian Pearce ('Historian' of the Socialist Labour League) in *Labour Review*, vol. V, No. 3.

Background

The Kronstadt insurrection broke out three months after the conclusion of the civil war on the European front.

As the Civil War drew to a victorious end the working masses of Russia were in a state of chronic famine. They were also increasingly dominated by a ruthless regime, ruled by a single party. The generation which had made October still remembered the promise of the social revolution and the hopes they had of building a new kind of society.

This generation had comprised a very remarkable section of the working class. It had reluctantly abandoned its demands for equality and for real freedom, believing them to be, if not incompatible with war, at least difficult to achieve under wartime conditions. But once victory was assured, the workers in the towns, the sailors, the Red Army men, and the peasants, all those who had shed their blood during the Civil War, could see no further justification for their hardships and for blind submission to a ferocious discipline. Even if these might have had some reason in wartime, such reasons no longer applied.

While many had been fighting at the front, others – those enjoying dominant positions in the State apparatus – had been consolidating their power and detaching themselves more and more from the workers. The bureaucracy was already assuming alarming proportions. The State machine was in the hands of a single Party, itself more and more permeated by careerist elements. A non Party worker was worth less, on the scale of everyday life, than an ex-bourgeois or nobleman, who had belatedly rallied to the Party. Free criticism no longer existed. Any Party member could denounce as 'counter revolutionary' any worker simply defending his class rights and his dignity as a worker.

Industrial and agricultural production were declining rapidly. There were virtually no raw materials for the factories. Machinery was worn and neglected. The main concern of the proletariat was the bitter fight against famine. Thefts from the factories had become a sort of compensation for miserably paid labour. Such thefts continued despite the repeated searches carried out by the Cheka at the factory gates.

Workers who still had connections with the countryside would go there to barter old clothes, matches or salt in exchange for food. The trains were crammed with such people (the *Mechotchniki*). Despite a thousand difficulties, they would try to bring food to the famished cities. Working class anger would break out repeatedly, as barrages of militia confiscated the paltry loads of flour or potatoes workers would be carrying on their backs to prevent their children from starving.

The peasants were submitted to compulsory requisitions. They were sowing less, despite the danger of famine that now resulted from bad crops. Bad crops had been common. Under ordinary conditions such crops had not automatically had these disastrous effects. The cultivated areas were larger and the peasants would usually set something aside for more difficult times.

The situation preceding the Kronstadt uprising can be summed up as a fantastic discrepancy between promise and achievement. There were harsh economic difficulties. But as important was the fact that the generation in question had not forgotten the meaning of the rights it had struggled for during the Revolution. This was to provide the real psychological background to the uprising.

The Red Navy had problems of its own. Since the Brest Litovsk peace, the Government had undertaken a complete reorganisation of the armed forces, on the basis of a rigid discipline, a discipline quite incompatible with the erstwhile principle of election of officers by the men. A whole hierarchical structure had been introduced. This had gradually stifled the democratic tendencies which had prevailed at the onset of the Revolution. For purely technical reasons such a reorganisation had not been possible in the Navy, where revolutionary traditions had strong roots. Most of the naval officers had gone over to the Whites, and the sailors still retained many of the democratic rights they had won in 1917. It had not been possible completely to dismantle their organisations.

This state of affairs was in striking contrast with what pertained in the rest of the armed forces. It could not last. Differences between the rank and file sailors and the higher command of the armed forces steadily increased. With the end of the Civil War in European Russia these differences became explosive.

Discontent was rampant not only among the non Party sailors. It also affected Communist sailors. Attempts to 'discipline' the Fleet by introducing 'Army customs' met with stiff resistance from 1920 on. Zef, a leading Party member and a member of the Revolutionary War Committee for the Baltic Fleet, was officially denounced by the Communist sailors for his 'dictatorial attitudes.' The enormous gap developing between the rank and file and the leadership was shown up during the elections to the Eighth Congress of Soviets, held in December 1920. At the naval base of Petrograd large numbers of sailors had noisily left the electoral meeting, openly protesting against the dispatch there as official delegates of people from Politotdiel and from Comflot (i.e., from the very organisations monopolising political control of the Navy).

On 15th February 1921, the Second Conference of Communist Sailors of the Baltic Fleet had met. It had assembled 300 delegates who had voted for the following resolutions:

'This Second Conference of Communist Sailors condemns the work of Poubalt (Political Section of the Baltic Fleet).

1. Poubalt has not only separated itself from the masses but also from the active functionaries. It has become transformed into a bureaucratic organ enjoying no authority among the sailors.

2. There is a total absence of plan or method in the work of Poubalt. There is also a lack of agreement between its actions and the resolutions adopted at the Ninth Party Congress.

3. Poubalt, having totally detached itself from the Party masses, has destroyed all local initiative. It has transformed all political work into paper work. This has had harmful repercussions on the organisation of the masses in the Fleet. Between June and November last year, 20 per cent of the (sailor) Party members have left the Party. This can be explained by the wrong methods of the work of Poubalt.

4. The cause is to be found in the very principles of Poubalts organisation. These principles must be changed in the direction of greater democracy.'

Several delegates demanded in their speeches the total abolition of the 'political sections' in the Navy, a demand we will find voiced again in the sailors' resolutions during the Kronstadt uprising. This was the frame of mind in which the famous discussion on the trade union question preceding the Tenth Party Congress took place.

In the documents of the period one can clearly perceive the will of certain Bolshevik leaders (amongst whom Trotsky) not only to ignore the great discontent affecting the workers and all those who had fought in the previous period, but also to apply military methods to the problems of everyday life, particularly to industry and to the trade unions.

In these heated discussions, the sailors of the Baltic Fleet adopted a viewpoint very different from Trotsky's. At the elections to the Tenth Party Congress, the Baltic Fleet voted solidly against its leaders: Trotsky, Peoples Commissar of War (under whose authority the Navy came), and Raskolnikov, Chief of the Baltic Fleet. Trotsky and Raskolnikov were in agreement on the Trade Union question.

The sailors sought to protest against the developing situation by abandoning the Party en masse. According to information released by Sorine, Commissar for Petrograd, 5,000 sailors left the Party in January 1921 alone.

There is no doubt that the discussion taking place within the Party at this time had profound effects on the masses. It overflowed the narrow limits the Party sought to impose on it. It spread to the working class as a whole, to the solders and to the sailors. Heated local criticism acted as a general catalyst. The proletariat had reasoned quite logically: if discussion and criticism were permitted to Party members, why should they not be permitted to the masses themselves who had endured all the hardships of the Civil War?

In his speech to the Tenth Congress – published in the Congress Proceedings – Lenin voiced his regret at having 'permitted' such a discussion. 'We have certainly committed an error,' he said, 'in having authorised this debate. Such a discussion was harmful just before the Spring months that would be loaded with such difficulties.'

Petrograd on the Eve of Kronstadt

Despite the fact that the population of Petrograd had diminished by two thirds, the winter of 1920-21 proved to be a particularly hard one.

Food in the city had been scarce since February 1917 and the situation had deteriorated from month to month. The town had always relied on food stuffs brought in from other parts of the country. During the Revolution the rural economy was in crisis in many of these regions. The countryside could only feed the capital to a very small extent. The catastrophic condition of the railways made things even worse. The ever increasing antagonisms between town and country created further difficulties everywhere.

To these partly unavoidable factors must be added the bureaucratic degeneration of the administration and the rapacity of the State organs for food supply. Their role in feeding the population was actually a negative one. If the population of Petrograd did not die of hunger during this period, it was above all thanks to its own adaptability and initiative. It got food wherever it could!

Barter was practised on a large scale. There was still some food to be had in the countryside, despite the smaller area under cultivation. The peasant would exchange this produce for the goods he lacked: boots, petrol, salt, matches. The population of the towns would try and get hold of these commodities in any way it could. They alone had real value. It would take them to the country side. In exchange people would carry back a few pounds of flour or potatoes. As we have mentioned before, the few trains, unheated, would be packed with men carrying bags on their shoulders. En route, the trains would often have to stop because they had run out of fuel. Passengers would get off and cut logs for the boilers.

Marketplaces had officially been abolished. But in nearly all towns there were semi tolerated illegal markets, where barter was carried out. Such markets existed in Petrograd. Suddenly, in the summer of 1920, Zinoviev issued a decree forbidding any kind of commercial transaction. The few small shops still open were closed and their doors sealed. However, the State apparatus was in no position to supply the towns. From this moment on, famine could no longer be attenuated by the initiative of the population. It became extreme. In January 1921, according to information published by Petrokommouns (the State Supplies of the town of Petrograd), workers in metal smelting factories were allocated rations of 800 grams of black bread a day; shock workers in other factories 600 grams; workers with A.V. cards: 400 grams; other workers: 200 grams. Black bread was the staple diet of the Russian people at this time.

But even these official rations were distributed irregularly and in even smaller amounts than those stipulated. Transport workers would receive, at irregular intervals, the equivalent of 700 to 1,000 calories a day. Lodgings were unheated. There was a great shortage of both clothing and footwear. According to official statistics, working class wages in 1920 in Petrograd were only 9 per cent. of those in 1913.

The population was drifting away from the capital. All who had relatives in the country had rejoined them. The authentic proletariat remained till the end, having the most slender connections with the countryside.

This fact must be emphasised, in order to nail the official lies seeking to attribute the Petrograd strikes that were soon to break out to peasant elements, 'insufficiently steeled in proletarian ideas.' The real situation was the very opposite. A few workers were seeking refuge in the countryside. The bulk remained. There was certainly no exodus of peasants into the starving towns! A few thousand 'Troudarmeitzys' (soldiers of the labour armies), then in Petrograd, did not modify the picture. It was the famous Petrograd proletariat, the proletariat which had played such a leading role in both previous revolutions, that was finally to resort to the classical weapon of the class struggle: the strike.

The first strike broke out at the Troubotchny factory, on 23rd February 1921. On the 24th, the strikers organised a mass demonstration in the street. Zinoviev sent detachments of 'Koursanty' (student officers) against them. The strikers tried to contact the Finnish Barracks. Meanwhile, the strikes were spreading. The Baltisky factory stopped work. Then the Laferma factory and a number of others: the Skorokhod shoe factory, the Admiralteiski factory, the Bormann and Metalischeski plants, and finally, on 28th February, the great Putilov works itself.

The strikers were demanding measures to assist food supplies. Some factories were demanding the re-establishment of the local markets, freedom to travel within a radius of thirty miles of the city, and the withdrawal of the militia detachments holding the road around the town. But side by side with these economic demands, several factories were putting forward more political demands; freedom of speech and of the press, the freeing of working class political prisoners. In several big factories, Party spokesmen were refused a hearing.

Confronted with the misery of the Russian workers who were seeking an outlet to their intolerable conditions, the servile Party Committee and Zinoviev, (who according to numerous accounts was behaving in Petrograd like a real tyrant), could find no better methods of persuasion than brute force.

Poukhov,[1] 'official' historian of the Kronstadt revolt, wrote that 'decisive class measures were needed to overcome the enemies of the revolution who were using a non class conscious section of the proletariat, in order to wrench power from the working class and its vanguard, the Communist Party"

On 24th February, the Party leaders set up a special General Staff, called the Committee of Defence. It was composed of three people: Lachevitch, Anzelovitch and Avrov. They were to be supported by a number of technical assistants. In each district of the town, a similar Committee of Three ('troika') was to be set up, composed of the local Party organiser, the commander of the Party battalion of the local territorial brigade and of a Commissar from the Officers' Training Corps. Similar Committees were organised in the outlying districts. These were composed of the local Party organiser, the President of the Executive of the local Soviet and the military Commissar for the District.

On 24th February the Committee of Defence proclaimed a state of siege in Petrograd. All circulation on the streets was forbidden after 11pm, as were all meetings and gatherings, both out of doors and indoors, that had not been specifically permitted by the Defence Committee. 'All infringements would be dealt with according to military law.' The decree was signed by Avrov (later shot by the Stalinists), Commander of the Petrograd military region, by Lachevitch (who later committed suicide), a member of the War Council, and by Bouline (later shot by the Stalinists), Commander of the forti-fied Petrograd District.

A general mobilisation of party members was decreed. Special detachments were created, to be sent to 'special destin-

---

1   Poukhov: *The Kronstadt Rebellion of 1921*. State Publishing House. 'Young Guard' edition, 1931. In the series: 'Stages of the Civil War'.

ations'. At the same time, the militia detachments guarding the roads in and out of the town were withdrawn. Then the strike leaders were arrested.

On 26th February the Kronstadt sailors, naturally interested in all that was going on in Petrograd, sent delegates to find out about the strikes. The delegation visited a number factories. It returned to Kronstadt on the 28th. That same day, the crew of the battleship 'Petropavlovsk,' having discussed the situation, voted the following resolution:[2]

> 'Having heard the reports of the representatives sent by the General Assembly of the Fleet to find out about the situation in Petrograd, the sailors demand:
>
> 1.   Immediate new elections to the Soviets. The present Soviets no longer express the wishes of the workers and peasants. The new elections should be by secret ballot, and should be preceded by free electoral propaganda.
> 2.   Freedom of speech and of the press for workers and peasants, for the Anarchists, and for the Left Socialist parties.
> 3.   The right of assembly, and freedom for trade union and peasant organisations.
> 4.   The organisation, at the latest on 10th March 1921, of a Conference of non-Party workers, solders and sailors of Petrograd, Kronstadt and the Petrograd District.

---

2   This resolution was subsequently endorsed by all the Kronstadt sailors in General Assembly, and by a number of groups of Red Army Guards. It was also endorsed by the whole working population of Kronstadt in General Assembly. It became the political programme of the insurrection. It therefore deserves a careful analysis.

5. The liberation of all political prisoners of the Socialist parties, and of all imprisoned workers and peasants, soldiers and sailors belonging to working class and peasant organisations.

6. The election of a commission to look into the dossiers of all those detained in prisons and concentration camps.

7. The abolition of all political sections in the armed forces. No political party should have privileges for the propagation of its ideas, or receive State subsidies to this end. In the place of the political sections various cultural groups should be set up, deriving resources from the State.

8. The immediate abolition of the militia detachments set up between towns and countryside.

9. The equalisation of rations for all workers, except those engaged in dangerous or unhealthy jobs.

10. The abolition of Party combat detachments in all military groups. The abolition of Party guards in factories and enterprises. If guards are required, they should be nominated, taking into account the views of the workers.

11. The granting to the peasants of freedom of action on their own soil, and of the right to own cattle, provided they look after them themselves and do not employ hired labour.

12. We request that all military units and officer trainee groups associate themselves with this resolution.

13. We demand that the Press give proper publicity to this resolution.

14. We demand the institution of mobile workers' control groups.

15. We demand that handicraft production be authorised provided it does not utilise wage labour.'

Analysis of the Kronstadt Programme

The Kronstadt sailors and the Petrograd strikers knew quite well that Russia's economic status was at the root of the political crisis. Their discontent was caused both by the famine and by the whole evolution of the political situation. The Russian workers were increasingly disillusioned in their greatest hope: the Soviets. Daily they saw the power of a single Party substituting itself for that of the Soviets. A Party, moreover, which was degenerating rapidly through the exercise of absolute power, and which was already riddled with careerists. It was against the monopoly exercised by this Party in all fields of life that the working class sought to react.

Point one of the Kronstadt resolution expressed an idea shared by the best elements of the Russian working class. Totally 'bolshevised' Soviets no longer reflected the wishes of the workers and peasants. Hence the demand for new elections, to be carried out according to the principle of full equality for all working class political tendencies.

Such a regeneration of the Soviets would imply the granting to all working class tendencies of the possibility for expressing themselves freely, without fear of calumny or extermination. Hence, quite naturally, there followed the idea of freedom of expression, of the Press, of Assembly and of organisation, contained in Point two.

We must stress that by 1921 the class struggle in the countryside had been fought to a virtual standstill. The vast majority of the kulaks had been dispossessed. It is quite wrong to claim that the granting of basic freedoms to the peasants –

as demanded in Point three – would have meant restoring political rights to the kulaks. It was only a few years later that the peasants were exhorted to 'enrich themselves' – and this by Bukharin, then an official Party spokesman.

The Kronstadt revolution had the merit of stating things openly and clearly. But it was breaking no new ground. Its main ideas were being discussed everywhere. For having, in one way or another, put forward precisely such ideas, workers and peasants were already filling the prisons and the recently set up concentration camps. The men of Kronstadt did not desert their comrades. Point six of their resolution shows that they intended to look into the whole juridical apparatus. They already had serious doubts as to its objectivity as an organ of their rule. The Kronstadt sailors were thereby showing a spirit of solidarity in the best working class tradition. In July 1917, Kerensky had arrested a deputation of the Baltic Fleet that had come to Petrograd. Kronstadt had immediately sent a further deputation to insist on their release. In 1921, this tradition was being spontaneously renewed.

Points seven and ten of the resolution attacked the political monopoly being exercised by the ruling Party. The Party was using State funds in an exclusive and uncontrolled manner to extend its influence both in the Army and in the police.

Point nine of their resolution demanded equal rations for all workers. This destroys Trotsky's accusation of 1938[3] according to which 'the men of Kronstadt wanted privileges, while the country was hungry.'

Point fourteen clearly raised the question of workers control. Both before and during the October Revolution this demand had provoked powerful echo among the working

---

3   The accusation was made in answer to a question put to Trotsky by Wedelin Thomas, a member of the New York Commission of Enquiry into the Moscow Trials.

class. The Kronstadt sailors understood quite clearly that real control had escaped from the hands of the rank and file. They sought to bring it back. The Bolshevik meanwhile sought to vest all control in the hands of a special Commissariat, the Rabkrin – Workers and Peasants inspection.[4]

Point eleven reflected the demands of the peasants to whom the Kronstadt sailors had remained linked – as had, as a matter of fact, the whole of the Russian proletariat. The basis of this link is to be found in the specific history of Russian industry. Because of feudal backwardness, Russian industry did not find its roots in petty handicraft. In their great majority, the Russian workers came directly from the peasantry. This must be stressed. The Baltic sailors of 1921 were, it is true, closely linked with the peasantry. But neither more so nor less than had been the sailors of 1917.

In their resolution, the Kronstadt sailors were taking up once again one of the big demands of October. They were supporting those peasant claims demanding the land and the right to own cattle for those peasants who did not exploit the

---

4   Whom has history vindicated in this matter? Shortly before his second stroke, Lenin was to write (*Pravda*, 28th January, 1923): 'Let us speak frankly. The Inspection now enjoys no authority whatsoever. Everybody knows that there is no worse institution than our Inspection'. This was said a bare eighteen months after the suppression of Kronstadt. (It is worth pointing out that Stalin had been the chief of the Rabkrin from 1919 till the spring of 1922, when he became General Secretary of the Party. He continued to exercise a strong influence over Rabkrin even after he had formally left it. Lenin, incidentally, had voiced no objection to Stalin's appointment or activities in this post. That only came later. Lenin had in fact defended both Stalin and Rabkrin against some of Trotsky's more far-sighted criticisms – see. I. Deutscher, *The Prophet Unarmed*, pp. 47-48. (Note added in 'Solidarity', Vol. 2, No. 7, p. 27).

labour of others. In 1921, moreover, there was another aspect to this particular demand. It was an attempt to solve the food question, which was becoming desperate. Under the system of forced requisition, the population of the towns was literally dying of hunger. Why, incidentally, should the satisfaction of these demands be deemed 'tactically correct' when advocated by Lenin, in March 1921, and 'counter revolutionary' when put forward by the peasants themselves a few weeks earlier?

What was so counter revolutionary about the Kronstadt programme. What could justify the crusade launched by the Party against Kronstadt? A workers and peasants' regime that did not wish to base itself exclusively on lies and terror, had to take account of the peasantry. It need not thereby have lost its revolutionary character. The men of Kronstadt were not alone, moreover, in putting forward such demands. In 1921, Makhno's followers were still active in the Ukraine. This revolutionary peasant movement was evolving its own ideas and methods of struggle. The Ukrainian peasantry had played a predominant role in chasing out the feudal hordes. It had earned the right itself to determine the forms of its social life.

Despite Trotsky's categorical and unsubstantiated assertions, the Makhno movement was in no sense whatsoever a kulak movement. Koubanin, the official Bolshevik historian of the Makhno movement, shows statistically, in a book edited by the Party's Historical institute, that the Makhno movement at first appeared and developed most rapidly, in precisely those areas where the peasants were poorest. The Makhno movement was crushed before it had a chance of showing in practice its full creative abilities. The fact that during the Civil War it had been capable of creating its own specific forms of struggle, leads one to guess that it could have been capable of a lot more.

The Kronstadt Uprising

As a matter of fact, in relation to agrarian policy, nothing was to prove more disastrous than the zigzags of the Bolsheviks. In 1931, ten years after Kronstadt, Stalin was to decree his famous 'liquidation of the kulaks.' This resulted in an atrocious famine and in the loss of millions of human lives.

Let us finally consider Point fifteen of the Kronstadt resolution, demanding freedom for handicraft production. This was not a question of principle. For the workers of Kronstadt, handicraft production was to compensate for an industrial production that had fallen to nought. Through this demand they were seeking a way out of their intolerable economic plight.

Mass Meetings

The Kronstadt Soviet was due to be renewed on 2nd March.

A meeting of the First and Second Battleship Sections had been planned for 1st. March. The notification had been published in the official journal of the city of Kronstadt. The speakers were to include Kalinin, President of the All Russian Executive of Soviets, and Kouzmin, political commissar to the Baltic Fleet. When Kalinin arrived, he was received with music and flags. All military honours were accorded him.

Sixteen thousand people attended the meeting. Party member Vassiliev, president of the local soviet, took the chair. The delegates who had visited Petrograd the previous day gave their reports. The resolution adopted on 28th February by the crew of the battleship 'Petropavlovsk' was distributed. Kalinin and Kouzmin opposed the resolution. They proclaimed that 'Kronstadt did not represent the whole of Russia.'

Nevertheless, the mass assembly adopted the Petropavlovsk resolution. In fact only two people voted against it: Kalinin and Kouzmin!

The mass assembly decided to send a delegation of 30 workers to Petrograd to study the situation on the spot. It was also decided to invite delegates from Petrograd to visit Kronstadt, so that they would get to know what the sailors were really thinking. A further mass meeting was planned for the following day, grouping delegates from ships' crews, from the Red Army groups, from State institutions, from the dockyards and factories, and from the trade unions, to decide on the procedure of new elections to the local soviet. At the end of the meeting, Kalinin was allowed to regain Petrograd in all safety.

The following day, 2nd. March, the delegates meeting took place in the House of Culture. According to the official Kronstadt '*Izvestia*', the appointment of delegates had taken place properly. The delegates all insisted that the elections be carried out in a loyal and correct manner. Kouzmin and Vassiliev spoke first. Kouzmin stated that the Party would not relinquish power without a fight. Their speeches were so aggressive and provocative that the assembly ordered them to leave the meeting and put them under arrest. Other Party members were, however, allowed to speak at length during the debate.

The meeting of delegates endorsed by an overwhelming majority the Petropavlovsk resolution. It then got down to examining in detail the question of elections to the new soviet. These elections were to 'prepare the peaceful reconstruction of the Soviet regime.' The work was constantly interrupted by rumours, spreading through the assembly, to the effect that the Party was preparing to disperse the meeting by force. The situation was extremely tense.

The Provisional Committee

Because of the threatening speeches of the representatives of the State power – Kouzmin and Vassiliev – and fearing retaliation, the assembly decided to form a Provisional

Revolutionary Committee, to which it entrusted the administration of the town and the fortress. The Committee held its first session aboard the 'Petropavlovsk', the battleship in which Kouzmin and Vassiliev were being detained.

The leading body of the assembly of delegates all became members of the Provisional Revolutionary Committee. They were:

- Petritchenko, chief quartermaster of the battleship 'Petropavlovsk',
- Yakovenko, liaison telephonist to the Kronstadt section,
- Ossossov, boiler man in the battleship 'Sebastopol',
- Arkhipov, chief engineer,
- Perepelkin, electrician in the battleship 'Sebastopol',
- Patrouchev, chief electrician in the 'Petropavlovsk',
- Koupolov, head male nurse,
- Verchinin, sailor in the 'Sebastopol',
- Toukin, worker in the 'Electrotechnical' factory,
- Romanenko, docks maintenance worker,
- Orechin, headmaster of the Third Labour School,
- Valk, sawmill worker,
- Pavlov, worker in a marine mining shop,
- Boikev, head of the building section of the Kronstadt fortress,
- Kilgast, harbour pilot.

The majority of the members of the Provisional Revolutionary Committee were sailors with a long service. This contradicts the official version of the Kronstadt events, which seeks to attribute the leadership of the revolt to elements recently joining the Navy and having nothing in common with the heroic sailors of 1917-1919.

The first proclamation of the Provisional Revolutionary Committee stated: 'We are concerned to avoid bloodshed. Our aim is to create through the joint efforts of town and fortress the proper conditions for regular and honest elections to the new soviet.'

Later that day, under the leadership of the Provisional Revolutionary Committee, the inhabitants of Kronstadt occupied all strategic points in the town, taking over the State establishments, the Staff Headquarters, and the telephone and wireless buildings. Committees were elected in all battleships and regiments. At about 9:00pm, most of the forts and most detachments of the Red Army had rallied. Delegates coming from Oranienbaum had also declared their support for the Provisional Revolutionary Committee. That same day the '*Izvestia*' printshops were occupied.

On the morrow, 3rd March, the men of Kronstadt published the first issue of the '*Izvestia of the Provisional Revolutionary Committee*'.[5] In it one read: 'The Communist Party, master of the State, has detached itself from the masses. It has shown itself incapable of getting the country out of its mess. Countless incidents have recently occurred in Petrograd and Moscow which show clearly that the Party has lost the confidence of the working masses. The Party is ignoring working class demands because it believes that these demands are the result of counter revolutionary activity. In this the Party is making a profound mistake.'

Bolshevik Slanders
Meanwhile, Moscow Radio was broadcasting as follows:

'Struggle against the White Guard Plot.' And, 'Just like other White Guard insurrections, the mutiny of ex-Gen-

---

5   The entire life of this short-lived journal was reprinted as an appendix to a book *Pravda o Kronshtadte*, (The Truth about Kronstadt), published in Prague, in 1921.

eral Kozlovsky and the crew of the battleship 'Petropavlovsk' has been organised by Entente spies. This is
clear from the fact that the French paper '*Le Monde*' published the following message from Helsingfors two weeks
before the revolt of General Kozlovsky: 'We are informed
from Petrograd that as the result of the recent Kronstadt
revolt, the Bolshevik military authorities have taken a
whole series of measures to isolate the town and to prevent the soldiers and sailors of Kronstadt from entering
Petrograd.'

'It is therefore clear that the Kronstadt revolt is being
led from Paris. The French counter espionage is mixed
up in the whole affair. History is repeating itself. The
Socialist Revolutionaries, who have their headquarters in
Paris, are preparing the ground for an insurrection
against the Soviet power. The ground prepared, their real
master, the Tsarist general appeared. The history of
Koltchak, installing his power in the wake of that of the
Socialist Revolutionaries, is being repeated.' (*Radio Stan-
zia Moskva* and *Radio Vestnik Rosta Moskva*, 3rd. March
1921.)

The two antagonists saw the facts differently. Their outlooks
were poles apart.

The call issued by Moscow's Radio was obviously coming
from the Politbureau's top leaders. It had Lenin's approval,
who must have been fully aware of what was happening at
Kronstadt. Even assuming that he had to rely on Zinoviev for
information, whom he knew to be cowardly and liable to
panic, it is difficult to believe that Lenin misunderstood the
real state of affairs. On 2nd. March, Kronstadt had sent an official delegation to see him. It would have been enough to cross
question it in order to ascertain the true situation.

Lenin, Trotsky, and the whole Party leadership knew quite well that this was no mere 'generals' revolt'. Why then invent this legend about General Kozlovsky, leader of the mutiny? The answer lies in the Bolshevik outlook, an outlook at times so blind that it could not see that lies were as likely to prove nefarious as to prove helpful. The legend of General Kozlovsky opened the path to another legend: that of the Wrangel officer allegedly conspiring with Trotsky in 1928-29. It in fact opened the path to the massive lying of the whole Stalin era.

Anyway, who was this General Kozlovsky, denounced by the official radio as the leader of the insurrection? He was an artillery general, and had been one of the first to defect to the Bolsheviks. He seemed devoid of any capacity as a leader. At the time of the insurrection he happened to be in command of the artillery at Kronstadt. The communist commander of the fortress had defected. Kozlovsky, according to the rules prevailing in the fortress, had to replace him. He, in fact, refused, claiming that as the fortress was now under the juris- diction of the Provisional Revolutionary Committee, the old rules no longer applied. Kozlovsky remained, it is true, in Kronstadt, but only as an artillery specialist. Moreover, after the fall of Kronstadt, in certain interviews granted to the Finnish press, Kozlovsky accused the sailors of having wasted precious time on issues other than the defence of the fortress. He explained this in terms of their reluctance to resort to bloodshed. Later, other officers of the garrison were also to accuse the sailors of military incompetence, and of complete lack of confidence in their technical advisers. Kozlovsky was the only general to have been present at Kronstadt. This was enough for the Government to make use of his name.

The men of Kronstadt did, up to a point, make use of the military know how of certain officers in the fortress at the time. Some of these officers may have given the men advice out of sheer hostility to the Bolsheviks. But in their attack on Kronstadt, the Government forces were also making use of ex-Tsarist officers. On the one side there were Kozlovsky, Salomi-anov, and Arkannihov; on the other, ex-Tsarist officers and specialists of the old regime, such as Toukhatchevsky, Kamenev, and Avrov. On neither side were these officers an independent force.

Effects on the Party Rank and File

On 2nd. March, the Kronstadt sailors, aware of their rights, their duties and the moral authority vested in them by their revolutionary past, attempted to set the soviets on a better path. They saw how distorted they had become through the dictatorship of a single party.

On 7th March, the Central Government launched its military onslaught against Kronstadt.

What had happened between these two dates?

In Kronstadt, the Provisional Revolutionary Committee, enlarged during a mass meeting by the co-option of five new members, had started to reorganise social life in both town and fortress. It decided to arm the workers of Kronstadt to ensure the internal protection of the town. It decreed the compulsory re-election, within three days, of the leading trade union committees and of the Congress of Trade Unions, in which bodies it wished to vest considerable powers.

Rank and file members of the Communist Party were showing their confidence in the Provisional Revolutionary Committee by a mass desertion from the Party. A number of them formed a Provisional Party Bureau which issued the following appeal:

'Give no credence to the absurd rumours spread by pro-vocateurs seeking bloodshed according to which responsible Party comrades are being shot or to rumours alleging that the Party is preparing an attack against Kronstadt. This is an absurd lie, spread by agents of the Entente, seeking to overthrow the power of the Soviets.

The Provisional Party Bureau considers re-elections to the Kronstadt Soviet to be indispensable. It calls on all its supporters to take part in these elections.

The Provisional Party Bureau calls on all its supporters to remain at their posts and to create no obstacles to the measures taken by the Provisional Revolutionary Committee. Long live the power of the Soviets! Long live international working class unity!

Signed (on behalf of the Provisional Party Bureau of Kronstadt): Iline (ex-commissar for supplies), Pervouchin (ex-President of the local Executive Committee), Kabanov (ex-President of the Regional Trade Union Bureau)'.

The Stalinist historian Poukhov referring to this appeal, declared that, 'it can only be considered a treasonable act and an opportunist step towards an agreement with the leaders of the insurrection, who are obviously playing a counter revolutionary role'.[6] Poukhov admits that this document had 'a certain effect' on the rank and file of the Party. According to him, 780 Party members in Kronstadt left the Party at this time!

Some of those resigning from the Party sent letters to the Kronstadt 'Izvestia', giving reasons for their action. The teacher Denissov wrote:

---

6   Poukhov: *The Kronstadt Rebellion of 1921*, in series 'Stages of the Civil War', p. 95. 'Young Guard' edition. 1931; State Publishing House. Moscow.

'I openly declare to the Provisional Revolutionary Committee that as from gunfire directed at Kronstadt, I no longer consider myself a member of the Party. I support the call issued by the workers of Kronstadt. All power to the Soviets, not to the Party!'

A military group assigned to the special company dealing with discipline also issued a declaration:

'We, the undersigned, joined the Party believing it to express the wishes of the working masses. In fact the Party has proved itself an executioner of workers and peasants. This is revealed quite clearly by recent events in Petrograd. These events show up the face of the Party leaders. The recent broadcasts from Moscow show clearly that the Party leaders are prepared to resort to any means in order to retain power.

We ask that henceforth, we no longer be considered Party members. We rally to the call issued by the Kronstadt garrison in its resolution of 2nd. March. We invite other comrades who have become aware of the error of their ways, publicly to recognise the fact.

Signed: *Gutman,   Yefimov, Koudriatzev,   Andreev.* ('*Izvestia*' of the Provisional Revolutionary Committee, 7th March 1921)'.

The Communist Party members in the 'Rif' fort published the following resolution:

'During the last three years, many greedy careerists have flocked to our Party. This has given rise to bureaucracy and has gravely hampered the struggle for economic reconstruction.

Our Party has always faced up to the problem of the struggle against the enemies of the proletariat and of the working masses. We publicly declare that we intend to continue in the future our defence of the rights secured by the working class. We will allow no White Guard to take advantage of this difficult situation confronting the Republic of Soviets. At the first attempt directed against its power we will know how to retaliate.

We fully accept the authority of the Provisional Revolutionary Committee, which is setting itself the objective of creating soviets genuinely representing the proletarian and working masses.

Long live the power of the Soviets, the real defenders of working class rights.

Signed: the Chairman and Secretary of the meeting of Communists in Fort Rif' ('*Izvestia*' of the Provisional Revolutionary Committee. 7th March 1921.

Were such declarations forcibly extracted from Party members by the regime of terror directed against Party members allegedly reigning in Kronstadt at the time? Not a shred of evidence has been produced to this effect. *Throughout the whole insurrection not a single imprisoned Communist was shot.* And this despite the fact that among the prisoners were men responsible for the fleet such as Kouzmin and Batys. The vast majority of Communist Party members were in fact left entirely free.

In the '*Izvestia*' of the Provisional Revolutionary Committee for 7th March, one can read under the heading 'We are not seeking revenge', the following note:

'The prolonged oppression to which the Party dictatorship has submitted the workers has provoked a natural indignation among the masses. This has led, in certain places, to boycotts and sackings directed against the relatives of Party members.

This must not take place. We are not seeking revenge. We are only defending our interests as workers. We must act cautiously. We must only take action against those who sabotage or those who through lying propaganda seek to prevent a reassertion of working class power and rights'.

In Petrograd, however, humanist ideas of rather a different kind were prevailing. As soon as the arrests of Kouzmin and Vassiliev were learned, the Defence Committee ordered the arrests of the families of all Kronstadt sailors known to be living in Petrograd. A Government plane showered Kronstadt with leaflets saying:

> 'The Defence Committee announces that it has arrested and imprisoned the families of the sailors as hostages for the safety of communist comrades arrested by the Kronstadt mutineers. We refer specifically to the safety of Fleet Commissar Kouzmin, and Vassiliev, President of the Kronstadt Soviet. If a hair of their heads is touched, the hostages will pay with their lives'. ('*Izvestia*' of the Provisional Revolutionary Committee, 5th March 1921).

The Provisional Revolutionary Committee replied with the following radio message:

> 'In the name of the Kronstadt garrison, the Provisional Revolutionary Committee of Kronstadt insists on the liberation, within 24 hours, of the families of the workers, sailors and red soldiers arrested as hostages by the Petrograd Soviet.

The Kronstadt garrison assures you that in the city of Kronstadt, Party members are entirely free and that their families enjoy absolute immunity. We refuse to follow the example of the Petrograd Soviet. We consider such methods, even when conducted by ferocious hatred, as utterly shameful and degrading.

Signed: Petritchenko, sailor, President of the Provisional Revolutionary Committee; Kilgast, Secretary'.

To refute rumours according to which Party members were being ill-treated, the Provisional Revolutionary Committee set up a special Commission to investigate the cases of the imprisoned communists. In its issue of 4th March, the '*Izvestia*' of the Provisional Revolutionary Committee announced that a Party member would be attached to the Commission. It is doubtful if this body ever got to work, as two days later the bombardment of Kronstadt began. The Provisional Revolutionary Committee did, however, receive a Party delegation. It granted it permission to visit the prisoners in the 'Petropavlovsk'. The prisoners had even been allowed to hold meetings among themselves, and to edit a wall newspaper. (Zaikovski: '*Kronstadt from 1917 to 1921*')

There was no terror in Kronstadt. Under very difficult and tragic circumstances, the 'rebels' had done their utmost to apply the basic principles of working class democracy. If many rank and file communists decided to support the Provisional Revolutionary Committee, it was because this body expressed the wishes and aspirations of the working people. In retrospect, this democratic self assertion of Kronstadt may appear surprising. It certainly contrasted with the actions and frame of mind prevailing among the Party leaders in Petrograd and Moscow. They remained blind, deaf and totally lacking in understanding of what Kronstadt and the working masses of the whole of Russia really wanted.

The Kronstadt Uprising

Catastrophe could still have been averted during those tragic days: Why then did the Petrograd Defence Committee use such abusive language? The only conclusion an objective observer can come to is that it was done with the deliberate intention of provoking bloodshed, thereby 'teaching everyone a lesson' as to the need for absolute submission to the central power.

Threats and Bribes

On 5th March, the Petrograd Defence Committee issued a call to the rebels.

'You are being told fairy tales when they tell you that Petrograd is with you or that the Ukraine supports you. These are impertinent lies. The last sailor in Petrograd abandoned you when he learned that you were led by generals like Kozlovskv. Siberia and the Ukraine support the Soviet power. Red Petrograd laughs at the miserable efforts of a handful of White Guards and Socialist Revolutionaries. You are surrounded on all sides. A few hours more will lapse and then you will he compelled to surrender. Kronstadt has neither bread nor fuel. *If you insist, we will shoot you like partridges.*

At the last minute, all those generals, the Kozlovskvs, the Bourksers, and all that riff raff, the Petrichenkos, and the Tourins will flee to Finland, to the White guards. And you, rank and file soldiers and sailors, where will you go then? Don't believe them when they promise to feed you in Finland. Haven't you heard what happened to Wrangel's supporters? They were transported to Constantinople. There they are dying like flies, in their thousands, of hunger and disease. This is the fate that awaits you, unless you immediately take a grip of yourselves. Surrender Immediately! Don't waste a minute. Collect your weapons and come over to us. Disarm and arrest your criminal leaders, and in particular the Tsarist generals. Whoever surrenders immediately will be forgiven. Surrender now.

Signed: The Defence Committee'.

In reply to these threats from Petrograd, the Provisional Revolutionary Committee issued a final appeal.

'TO ALL, TO ALL, TO ALL.

Comrades, workers, red soldiers and sailors. Here in Kronstadt we know full well how much you and your wives and your children are suffering under the iron rule of the Party. We have overthrown the Party dominated Soviet. The Provisional Revolutionary Committee is today starting elections to a new Soviet. It will be freely elected, and it will reflect the wishes of the whole working population, and of the garrison – and not just those of a handful of Party members.

Our cause is just. We stand for the power of the Soviets, not for that of the Party. We stand for freely elected representatives of the toiling masses. Deformed Soviets, dominated by the Party, have remained deaf to our pleas. Our appeals have been answered with bullets.

The workers' patience is becoming exhausted. So now they are seeking to pacify you with crumbs. On Zinoviev's orders the militia barrages have been withdrawn. Moscow has allocated ten million gold roubles for the purchase abroad of food stuffs and other articles of first necessity. But we know that the Petrograd proletariat will not be bought over in this way. Over the heads of the Party, we hold out to you the fraternal hand of revolutionary Kronstadt.

Comrades, you are being deceived. And truth is being distorted by the basest of calumnies.

Comrades, don't allow yourselves to be misled.

In Kronstadt, power is in the hands of the sailors, of the red soldiers and of the revolutionary workers. It is not in the hands of white Guards commanded by General Kozlovsky, as Moscow Radio lyingly asserts.

Signed: The Provisional Revolutionary Committee'.

Foreign communists were in Moscow and Petrograd at the time of the revolt. They were in close contact with leading Party circles. They confirmed that the Government had made hasty purchases abroad (even chocolate was bought, which had always been a luxury in Russia). Moscow and Petrograd had suddenly changed their tactics. The Government had a better grasp of psychological war than had the men of Kronstadt. It understood the corrupting influence of white bread on a starving population. It was in vain that Kronstadt asserted that crumbs would not buy the Petrograd proletariat. The Government's methods had undoubted effect, especially when combined with vicious repression directed against the strikers.

Support in Petrograd

Part of the Petrograd proletariat continued to strike during the Kronstadt events. Poukhov, the Party historian, himself admits this. The workers were demanding the liberation of the prisoners. In certain factories, copies of the '*Izvestia*' of the Provisional Revolutionary Committee were found plastered on the walls. A lorry even drove through the street of Petrograd scattering leaflets from Kronstadt. In certain enterprises (for instance, the State Printing Works No. 26), the workers refused to adopt a resolution condemning the Kronstadt sailors. At the 'Arsenal' factory, the workers organised a mass meeting on 7th March, (the day the bombardment of Kronstadt began). This meeting adopted a resolution of the mutinous sailors! It elected a commission which was to go from factory to factory, agitating for a general strike.

Strikes were continuing in the biggest factories of Petrograd: Poutilov, Baltisky, Oboukhov, Nievskaia Manoufactura, etc. The authorities sacked the striking workers, transferred the factories to the authority of the local troikas (three men committees), who proceeded to selective rehiring of workers. Other repressive measures were also taken against the strikers.

Strikes were also starting in Moscow, in Nijni Novgorod and in other cities. But here too, the prompt delivery of food-stuffs, combined with calumnies to the effect that Tsarist generals were in command at Kronstadt had succeeded in sowing doubts among the workers.

The Bolsheviks' aim had been achieved. The proletariat of Petrograd and of the other industrial cities was in a state of confusion. The Kronstadt sailors, who had been hoping for the support of the whole of working class Russia, remained isolated, confronting a Government determined to annihilate them, whatever the cost.

First Skirmishes

On 6th March, Trotsky addressed an appeal by radio to the Kronstadt garrison:

'The Workers' and Peasants' Government has decided to reassert its authority without delay, both over Kronstadt and over the mutinous battleships, and to put them at the disposal of the Soviet Republic. I therefore order all those who have raised a hand against the Socialist Fatherland, immediately to lay down their weapons. Those who resist will be disarmed and put at the disposal of the Soviet Command. The arrested commissars and other representatives of the Government must be freed immediately.

Only those who surrender unconditionally will be able to count on the clemency of the Soviet Republic. I am meanwhile giving orders that everything be prepared to smash the revolt and the rebels by force of arms. The responsibility for the disasters which will effect the civilian population must fall squarely on the heads of the White Guard insurgents.

Signed: Trotsky, President of the Military Revolutionary Council of the Soviet Republic, KAMENEV,[7] Glavkom (Commanding Officer)'.

On 8th March, a plane flew over Kronstadt and dropped a bomb. On the following days, Government artillery continued to shell the fortress and neighbouring forts, but met with stiff resistance. Aircraft dropped bombs which provoked such fury among the civilian population that they started firing back. The Provisional Revolutionary Committee had to order the defenders not to waste their ammunition.

By 1921 the Kronstadt garrison had been markedly reduced. Figures issued by the General Staff of the defenders put the number at 3,000. Gaps between infantrymen defending the perimeter were at least 32 feet wide. Stocks of ammunition and shells were also limited.

During the afternoon of 3rd. March, the Revolutionary Committee had met in conference together with certain military specialists. A Military Defence Committee was set up which prepared a plan to defend the fortress. But when the military advisers proposed an assault in the direction of Oranienbaum (where there were food stocks, at Spassatelnaia), the Provisional Revolutionary Committee refused. It was not

---

7   This Kamenev was an ex-Tsarist officer, now collaborating with the Soviet Government. He was a different Kamenev from the one shot by the Stalinists in 1936.

putting its faith in the military capacity of the sailors; but in the moral support of the whole of proletarian Russia. Until the first shot had been fired, the men of Kronstadt refused to believe that the Government would militarily attack them. This is no doubt why the Provisional Revolutionary Committee had not set out to prevent the approach of the Red Army by breaking the ice around the foot of the fortress. For much the same reasons, fortified barrages were not set up along the probable line of attack.

Kronstadt was right. Militarily they could not win. At best, they could have held a fortnight. This might have been important, for once the ice had melted, Kronstadt could have become a real fortress, capable of defending itself. Nor must we forget that their human reserves were infinitesimal, compared with the numbers the Red Army could throw into battle.

Demoralisation in the Red Army

What was morale like in the Red Army at this time? In an interview given to 'Krasnaia Gazeta', Dybenko[8] described how all the military units participating in the assault on Kronstadt had to be reorganised. This was an absolute necessity. During the first day of military operations, the Red Army had shown that it did not wish to fight against the sailors, against the 'bratichki' (little brothers), as they were known at the time. Amongst the advanced workers, the Kronstadt sailors were known as people most devoted to the Revolution. And anyway, the very motives that were driving Kronstadt to revolt, existed among the ranks of the Red Army. Both were

---

8   Old Bolshevik. President of the Tsentrobalt (Central Committee of the Sailors of the Baltic Fleet) in July 1917. After October Revolution member of the First Soviet of Peoples' Commissars. Together with Antonov Ovseenko and Krylenko was put in charge of Army and Navy.

hungry and cold, poorly clad and poorly shod and this was no mean burden in the Russian winter, especially when what was asked of them was to march and fight on ice and snow.

During the night of 8th March, when the Red Army attack against Kronstadt started, a terrible snow storm was blowing over the Baltic. Thick fog made the tracks almost invisible. The Red Army soldiers wore long white blouses which hid them well against the snow. This is how Poukhov[9] described morale in Infantry Regiment 561 in an official communique. The regiment was approaching Kronstadt from the Oranienbaum side.

'At the beginning of the operation the second battalion had refused to march. With much difficulty and thanks to the presence of communists, it was persuaded to venture on the ice. As soon as it reached the first south battery, a company of the 2nd. battalion surrendered. The officers had to return alone. The regiment stopped. Dawn was breaking. We were without news of the 3rd. battalion, which was advancing towards south batteries 1 and 2. The battalion was marching in file and was being shelled by artillery from the forts. It then spread out and veered to the left of Fort Milioutine, from which red flags were being waved. Having advanced a further short distance, it noticed that the rebels had fitted machine guns on the forts, and were offering them the choice of surrendering or being massacred. Everybody surrendered, except the battalion commissar and three or four soldiers who turned back on their steps'.

On 8th March, Oublanov, Commissar for the Northern Sector, wrote to the Petrograd Party:

---

9   op. cit.

'I consider it my revolutionary duty to clarify you as to the state of affairs on the northern sector. It is impossible to send the Army into a second attack on the forts. I have already spoken to Comrades Lachevitch, Avrov and Trotsky about the morale of the Koursantys (cadet officers, deemed most fit for battle). I have to report the following tendencies. The men wish to know the demands of Kronstadt. They want to send delegates to Kronstadt. The number of political commissars in this sector is far from sufficient'.

Army morale was also revealed in the case of the 79th Brigade of the 27th Omsk Division. The Division comprised three regiments. It had shown its fighting capacities in the struggle against Koltchak. On 12th March, the division was brought to the Kronstadt front. The Orchane regiment refused to fight against Kronstadt. The following day, in the two other regiments of the same division, the soldiers organised impromptu meetings where they discussed what attitude to take. Two of the regiments had to be disarmed by force, and the 'revolutionary' tribunal imposed heavy sentences.

There were many similar cases. Not only were the soldiers unwilling to fight against their class brothers, but they were not prepared to fight on the ice in the month of March. Units had been brought in from other regions of the country, where by mid March the ice was melting already. They had little confidence in the solidity of the Baltic ice. Those who had taken part in the first assault, had seen that the shells from Kronstadt were opening up enormous holes in its surface, in which the unfortunate Government troops were being engulfed. These were hardly encouraging scenes. All this contributed to the failure of the first assaults against Kronstadt.

Reorganisation

The regiments to be used in the final assault against Kronstadt were thoroughly reorganised. Groups that had shown any sympathy towards Kronstadt were disarmed and transferred to other units. Some were severely punished by the Revolutionary Tribunal. Party members were mobilised and allocated to various battalions for purposes of propaganda and for reporting back on unsure elements.

Between 8th and 15th of March, while the cannons exchanged fire over the ice at Kronstadt, the Tenth Party Congress was held in Moscow. The Congress despatched 300 delegates to the front, among them Vorochilov, Boubnov, Zatousky, Roukhimovitch and Piatakov. The 'delegates' were nominated 'political commissars' and appointed to the military section of the Tcheka, or to 'special commissions for the struggle against desertion'. Some just fought in the ranks.

The Revolutionary Tribunals were working overtime. Poukhov describes how 'they would vigorously react to all unhealthy tendencies. Troublemakers and provocateurs were punished according to their deserts'. The sentences would immediately be made known to the soldiers. Some times they would even be published in the papers.

But despite all the propaganda, all the reorganisation, and all the repression, the soldiers retained their doubts. On 14th March, there were further acts of insubordination. Regiment 561, reorganised on 8th March, still refused to march. 'We will not fight against our brothers from the same 'stanltsas',[10] they proclaimed.

Small groups of Red Army men surrendered to the rebels and started fighting on their side. Witnesses described how some units lost half their men before even entering the line of

---

10   Cossack villages. Regiment 560, also composed of Cossacks and Ukraini-
ans, was fighting on the side of Kronstadt.

fire of the insurgents. They were being machined gunned from the rear 'to prevent them surrendering to the rebels'.

Official sources described how issues of the Kronstadt '*Izvestia*' were being read with great interest in the Red Army. So were the leaflets distributed by the Kronstadt rebels. Special political commissions were set up to prevent such material from entering the barracks. But this had an opposite effect from the one expected.

Party organisations throughout the country were mobilised. Intensive propaganda was carried out among the troops in the rear. The human and material resources available to the Government were far greater than those available to Kronstadt. Trains were daily bringing new troops to Petrograd. Many were being sent from the Kirghiz and Bachkir lands (i.e., were composed of men as far removed as possible from the 'Kronstadt frame of mind'). As to the defenders of Kronstadt, their forces were not only diminishing numerically (through losses sustained in fighting), but they were more and more exhausted. Badly clad and half starving, the Kronstadt rebels remained at their guns, almost without relief, for just over a week. At the end of this period, many of them could hardly stand.

The Final Assault

Aware of these facts and having taken all necessary measures in relation to organisation, supplies and improvement in morale Toukhatchevsky, commander of the 7th Army, issued his famous proclamation of 15th March. He ordered that Kronstadt be taken by all out assault in the night of 16th-17th March. Entire regiments of the 7th Army were equipped with hand grenades, white blouses, shears for cutting barbed wire and with small sleighs for carrying machine guns.

Toukhatchevsky's plan was to launch a decisive attack from the south, and then to capture Kronstadt by a massive simultaneous assault from three different directions.

On 16th March, the Southern Group opened its artillery barrage at 14.20 hrs. At 17.00 hrs. the Northern Group also started shelling Kronstadt. The Kronstadt guns answered back. The bombardment lasted four hours. Aircraft then bombed the city, with a view to creating panic among the civilian population. In the evening, the artillery bombardment ceased. The Kronstadt searchlights swept over the ice looking for the invaders.

Towards midnight, the Government troops had taken up their position and started to advance. At 2:45am, the Northern Force had occupied Fort 7, abandoned by the Kronstadt defenders. At 4:30am, Government troops attacked Forts 4 and 6, but suffered very heavy losses from the Kronstadt artillery. At 6:40am, Government officer cadets finally captured Fort 6.

At 5:00am, the Southern Force launched an attack on the forts facing them. The defenders, overwhelmed, fell back towards the city. A fierce and bloody battle then broke out in the streets. Machine guns were used, at very close range. The sailors defended each house, each attic, each shed. In the town itself, they were reinforced by the workers' militias. The attacking troops were, for a few hours, thrown back towards the forts and suburbs. The sailors reoccupied the Mechanical Institute, which had been captured early by the 80th government Brigade.

The street fighting was terrible. Red Army soldiers were losing their officers, Red Army men and defending troops were mixing in indescribable confusion. No one quite knew who was on which side. The civilian population of the town tried to fraternise with the Government troops, despite the shooting. Leaflets of the Provisional Revolutionary Committee were still being distributed. To the bitter end the sailors were trying to fraternise.

Throughout 17th March the fighting raged on. By the evening the Northern Group had occupied most of the forts. Street fighting continued throughout the night and well into the following morning. One by one the last forts – Milioutine, Constantine and Obroutchev – fell. Even after the last one had been occupied, isolated groups of defenders were still desperately fighting back with machine guns. Near the Tolbukhin light house, a final group of 150 sailors put up a desperate resistance.

The Balance Sheet

Figures issued by the Military Health Authorities of the Petrograd District – and relating to the period between 3rd. and 21st. March – spoke of 4,127 wounded and 527 killed. These figures do not include the drowned, or the numerous wounded left to die on the ice.[11] Nor do they include the victims of the Revolutionary Tribunals.

We do not even have approximate figures as to the losses on the Kronstadt side. They were enormous, even without the reprisal massacres that later took place. Perhaps one day the archives of the Tcheka and of the Revolutionary Tribunals will reveal the full and terrible truth.

This is what Poukhov, 'official' Stalinist historian of the revolt, says on the matter: 'While steps were being taken to re-establish normal life, and as the struggle against rebel

---

11 So numerous were the latter that the Finnish Foreign Ministry started discussions with Bersine, the Russian ambassador, with a view to joint frontier guard patrols clearing the corpses from the ice. The Finns feared that hundreds of bodies would be washed on to the Finnish shores after the ice had melted.

remnants was being pursued, the Revolutionary Tribunals of the Petrograd Military District were carrying out their work in many areas' … 'Severe proletarian justice was being meted out to all traitors to the Cause' … 'The sentences were given much publicity in the press and played a great educational role'. These quotations from official sources refute Trotskyist lies that 'the fortress was surrounded and captured with insignificant losses.'[12]

In the night of 17th-18th March, part of the Provisional Revolutionary Committee left Kronstadt. Some 8,000 people (some sailors and the most active part of the civilian population), moved towards Finland and permanent exile. When the Red Army – defenders of the 'soviet' power – finally entered Kronstadt, they did not re-establish the Kronstadt soviet. Its functions were taken over by the Political Section of the Secretariat of the new Assistant Commander of the Fortress.

The whole Red Fleet was profoundly reorganised. Thousands of Baltic sailors were sent to serve in the Black Sea, in the Caspian and in Siberian naval stations. According to Poukhov: 'the less reliable elements, those infected with the Kronstadt spirit, were transferred. Many only went reluctantly. This measure contributed to the purification of an unhealthy atmosphere'.

In April, the new Naval Command started an individual check. 'A special commission dismissed 15,000 sailors in 'non essential' (i.e., non specialised) categories V, G, and D – as well as sailors not considered reliable from a political point of view'.

After the physical annihilation of Kronstadt, its very spirit had to be eradicated from the Fleet.

---

12 On 10th September 1937, Trotsky wrote in *La Lutte Ouvrière*, 'the legend that would have it that Kronstadt 1921 was a great massacre'.

What They Said at the Time

'Revolts by workers and peasants have shown that their patience has come to an end. The uprising of the workers is near at hand. The time has come to overthrow the bureaucracy... Kronstadt has raised for the first time the banner of the Third Revolution of the toilers... The autocracy has fallen. The Constituent Assembly has departed to the region of the damned. The bureaucracy is crumbling...' *Izvestia* of the Kronstadt Provisional Revolutionary Committee. Etapy Revoliutsi (Stages of the Revolution), March 12, 1921.

'In the bourgeois newspapers you can read that we brought up Chinese, Kalmuk and other regiments against Yudemitch and Kronstadt. This is, of course, a lie. We brought up our youth. The storming of Kronstadt was indeed symbolic. Kronstadt, as I said, was about to pass into the hands of French and English imperialism.' L. Trotsky. Speech delivered at 2nd Congress of Communist Youth International, July 14, 1921. *The First Five Years of The Communist International* (Pioneer Publishers, 1945), p. 312.

The Anarchists

Did the Kronstadt sailors put forward their demands and resolutions by themselves? Or were they acting under the influence of political groups, which might have suggested slogans to them? Anarchist influence is often incriminated when this subject is described. How sure can one be of the matter? Among members of the Provisional Revolutionary Committee, as among the Kronstadters in general, there were certainly individuals claiming to be anarchists. But if one bases oneself on documentary evidence, as we have sought to do throughout this study, one must conclude that there was no direct intervention by anarchist groups.

The Menshevik Dan, who was in prison for a while in Petrograd with a group of Kronstadt rebels, tells us in his memoirs[1] that Perepelkin, one of the members of the Provisional Revolutionary Committee, was close to anarchism. He also tells us that the Kronstadt sailors were both disillusioned and fed up with Communist Party policy and that they spoke with hatred about political parties in general. In their eyes, the Mensheviks and the Socialist Revolutionaries were as bad as the Bolsheviks. All were out to seize power and would later betray the people who had vested their confidence in them. According to Dan, the conclusion of the sailors, disappointed with political parties was: 'You are all the same. What we need is anarchism, not a power structure!'.

The anarchists of course defend the Kronstadt rebels. It seems likely to us that had any of their organisations really lent a hand in the insurrection the anarchist press would have mentioned the fact. In the anarchist press of the time, however, there is no mention of such help. For instance Yartchouk, an old anarcho-syndicalist[2] who before October had

---

1 Dan, T: *Two Years of Roaming* (1919-21) in Russian.

2 In 1926 he became a Communist and returned to Russia.

enjoyed considerable authority amongst the population and sailors of Kronstadt, mentions no such anarchist role in his pamphlet devoted to the 1921 uprising,[3] written immediately after the events. We must consider his judgement as fairly conclusive evidence.

At the time of the insurrection the anarchists were already being persecuted all over the country. Isolated libertarians and the few remaining anarchist groupings were undoubtedly 'morally' on the side of the insurgents. This is shown for instance in the following leaflet, addressed to the working class of Petrograd:

'The Kronstadt revolt is a revolution. Day and night you can hear the sound of the cannon. You hesitate to intervene directly against the Government to divert its forces from Kronstadt, although the cause of Kronstadt is your cause... The men of Kronstadt are always in the forefront of rebellion. After the Kronstadt revolt let us see the revolt of Petrograd. And after you, let anarchism prevail.'

Four anarchists then in Petrograd (Emma Goldman, Alexander Berkman, Perkous and Petrovsky) foresaw a bloody outcome to events. On March 5, they sent the following letter to the Petrograd Council for Labour and Defence:

'It is not only impossible but in fact criminal to keep quiet at the present time. Recent developments compel us anarchists to give our opinion on the present situation. The discontent and ferment in the minds of the workers and sailors are the result of circumstances which deserve serious attention from us. Cold and famine have provoked discontent, while the absence of any possibility of discussion or criticism drive the workers and sailors to seek an outlet to this discontent. The fact that a workers'

---

3   Yartchouk. *The Kronstadt Revolt*. In Russian and Spanish.

and peasants' government uses force against workers and sailors is even more important. It will create a reaction- ary impression in the international labour movement and will therefore harm the cause of the social revolution. Bolshevik comrades, think while there is still time. Don't play with fire. You are about to take a decisive step. We propose the following to you: nominate a commission of six, of which two should be anarchists, to go to Kronstadt to solve the differences peacefully. In the present circum- stances this is the most rational way of doing things. It will have an international revolutionary significance.'

These anarchists certainly did their duty. But they acted on their own and there is nothing to show that they were organ- isationally linked with the rebels in any way. Moreover the very fact that they proposed this kind of mediation suggests that they were not in direct contact with the sailors, who had themselves sent a deputation to Petrograd through which it would have been possible to negotiate. And if, in the 'Petro- pavlovsk' resolution, we find the demand of freedom of speech and freedom of publication for the anarchists, this merely shows that the Kronstadters of 1921 had retained their ideas and traditions of before October.

Before October both Bolsheviks and Anarchists had consid- erable influence at Kronstadt.[4] In the summer of 1917, at a meeting of the Petrograd Soviet, Trotsky had been able to answer the Menshevik leader Tseretelli:

'Yes, the Kronstadters are anarchists. But during the final stage of the Revolution the reactionaries who are now inciting you to exterminate Kronstadt will be preparing

---

4   According to the testimony of well-known Bolsheviks such as Flerovski and Raskolnikov.

ropes to hang both you and us. And it will be the Kronstadters who will fight to the last to defend us.'

The anarchists were well-known in Kronstadt as revolutionaries. That is why the rebels, when they spoke of opening the
doors of the Soviets to different socialist tendencies, had first
thought of the anarchists as well as of the left Socialist Revolutionaries.

The most important of the demands of the Petropavlovsk
resolution were those calling for democratic rights for the
workers and those peasants not exploiting the labour of others
and the demand calling for the abolition of the monopoly of
Party influence. These demands were part of the programme
of other socialist tendencies, already reduced to illegality. The
anarchists agreed with these demands and were not the only
ones to be putting them forward.

On the other hand the Kronstadters repeatedly insisted that
they were 'for soviet power'. A small minority of Russian libertarians (the 'soviet anarchists') were known to support the idea
of close collaboration with the soviets, which were already
integrated into the state machine. The Makhnovist movement
on the other hand (which was not exclusively anarchist
although under the strong personal influence of Makhno, an
anarchist since the age of 16) did not speak of 'soviet power' as
some thing to be defended. Its slogan was 'free soviets', i.e.
soviets where different political tendencies might coexist,
without being vested with state power.

The Kronstadters believed that the trade unions had an
important role to play. This idea was by no means an exclusively anarchist one. It was shared by the left Socialist
Revolutionaries and by the Workers' Opposition (Kollontal
and Chliapnikov) in the Communist Party itself. Later other
oppositional communist tendencies (like the Sapronovites)
were to espouse it. In short the idea was the hallmark of all

those who sought to save the Russian Revolution through proletarian democracy and through an opposition to the one-party monopoly which had started dominating and was now replacing all other tendencies.

We may conclude by saying that anarchism had an influence on the Kronstadt insurrection to the extent that it advocated the idea of proletarian democracy.

The Mensheviks

The Mensheviks had never carried much weight among the sailors. The number of Menshevik deputies to the Kronstadt Soviet bore no real relation to their influence in the Fleet. The anarchists, who after the second election only had three or four deputies to the Soviet, enjoyed a far greater popularity. This paradoxical situation arose from the lack of organisation among the anarchists and also from the fact that in 1917 the differences between bolshevism and anarchism were hardly perceptible to the masses. Many anarchists at that time saw bolshevism as a kind of Bakouninized Marxism.[5]

The Mensheviks – at least their official faction – although fundamentally hostile to Bolshevism, were not in favour of an armed struggle against the State power. Because of this they were hostile to armed intervention[6]. They tried to play the role of a legal opposition both in the Soviets and in the trade unions. Opposed both to the dictatorship of the proletariat and to the dictatorship of a single party and convinced that a stage of capitalist development still confronted Russia, they felt that armed interventions would only prevent the democratic

---

5   This idea was later developed by Hermann Sandomirski, a 'soviet anarchist', in an article published in the Moscow *Izvestia*, on the occasion of Lenin's death.

6   In fact during Denikin's offensive of 1919 they had told their members to enter the Red Army.

forces in Russia from establishing themselves. They hoped that once the armed struggle had come to an end the regime would be compelled to follow a course of democratic transformation.

On March 7, 1921, during the Kronstadt insurrection, the underground Petrograd Committee of the Mensheviks published the following leaflet:

'To the workers, red soldiers and Koursantys of Petrograd.

Stop the slaughter! The guns are thundering and the Communists who claim to be a Workers Party are shooting the sailors of Kronstadt.

We don't know all the details about what has happened at Kronstadt. But we do know that the Kronstadters have called for free elections to the soviets and for the release of arrested socialists and of arrested non-party workers and soldiers. They have called for the convening, on March 10, of a non-party conference of workers, red soldiers and sailors to discuss the critical situation of Soviet Russia.

A genuine workers' power should have been able to clarify the real causes of the Kronstadt events. It should have discussed things openly with the workers and sailors of Kronstadt, in front of the whole of working class Russia. Instead, the Bolsheviks have proclaimed a state of siege and have machine-gunned the soldiers and sailors.

Comrades, we cannot, we must not just sit and listen to the sound of the guns. Each salvo may destroy dozens of human lives. We must intervene and put an end to this massacre.

Insist that military operations against the sailors and workers of Kronstadt be ended immediately. Insist that the Government start immediate negotiations with Kronstadt, with the participation of Petrograd factory delegates. Elect delegates forthwith to participate in these discussions. Stop the slaughter!'

The Central Committee of the Mensheviks had also published a leaflet. This proclaimed that 'what was necessary was not a policy of violence towards the peasantry but a policy of conciliation towards it. Power should really be in the hands of the working masses. To this end new and free elections to the soviets were essential. What was needed was that Workers' Democracy, much talked about but of which one couldn't see the slightest trace.'

Sozialistitchenski Vestnik, the official organ of Russian Social Democracy (published abroad) assessed the Kronstadt insurrection as follows: 'It is precisely the masses themselves, who until now had supported bolshevism, who have now taken the initiative in a decisive struggle against the present regime'. The paper considered the Kronstadt slogans to be Menshevik ones and added that Mensheviks 'had all the greater right to be pleased about it, in view of the fact that their party had played no role in the insurrection, given the total lack of any Menshevik organisation in the Fleet'.

Martov, the leader of Russian Menshevism was already out of Russia. In an article in *Freiheit*, published on May 1st 1921, he denied that either Mensheviks or Social Revolutionaries had played any part in the insurrection. The initiative, he felt, was coming from the sailors who were breaking with the Communist Party at the organisational level, but not at the level of principles.

Poukhov quotes another leaflet signed by one of the numerous groups of Mensheviks. It said: 'Down with the lies of the Counter Revolution! Where are the real counter-revolutionaries? They are the Bolsheviks, the commissars. those who speak of 'soviet power'. Against them the real Revolution is rising up. We must support it. We must come to the rescue of

Kronstadt. Our duty is to help Kronstadt. Long live the Revolution. Long live the Constituent Assembly!' The Menshevik Central Committee declined all responsibility for slogans put forward by such dissident groupings.

The Right SRs

The call for the convening of the Constituent Assembly was the central theme of the propaganda of the Right wing Socialist Revolutionaries. In *Revolutzionaia Rossia*, their Party organ (which in March 1921 was being published abroad) Victor Tchernov, ex-president of the dissolved Constituent Assembly and leader of the Right SRs wrote: 'All those who want to find a way out of the disgusting, bloodstained Bolshevik dictatorship, all those who wish to tread the path of freedom must stand up around Kronstadt and come to its help. The crown of democracy must be the Constituent Assembly'.

Now Tchernov was fully aware that in No. 6 of the *Kronstadt Izvestia* the rebel sailors had written 'The workers and peasants will go forward. *They will leave behind them the Utchred-Nika* (pejorative form for the Constituent Assembly) *and its bourgeois regime. They will also leave behind them the Communist Party dictatorship with its tchekas and its State Capitalism*, which has seized the masses by the throat and is threatening to throttle them'. When Tchernov discussed these lines of the Kronstadters he attributed them to an ideological survival of past Bolshevik influence.

By personal and political temperament, Tchernov was diametrically opposed to the Mensheviks. With his political friends he launched a passionate appeal to the sailors.

'The Bolsheviks killed the cause of liberty and democracy when they counterposed, in the popular mind, the idea of soviets to the idea of the Constituent Assembly.

Instead of seeing the soviets as a support for the Constituent Assembly, as a powerful link between the Assembly and the country, they raised the soviets against the Assembly and thereby killed both the soviets and the Assembly. This is what you must understand, deceived workers, soldiers, and sailors. Let your slogan 'free elections to the soviets' reverberate, as a call to a march from the soviets to the Constituent Assembly.'

Tchernov went even further. From a private ship he sent the following radio message to the Provisional Revolutionary Committee:

'The President of the Constituent Assembly, Victor Tchernov, sends fraternal greetings to the heroic sailor, soldier and worker comrades who, for the third time since 1905, are shaking off the yoke of tyranny. Acting as an intermediary, he proposes, with the help of Russian co-operative organisations now abroad, to send men to ensure the feeding of Kronstadt. Let me know what you need and how much you need. I am prepared to come personally and to place both my forces and my authority at the disposal of the popular revolution. I have confidence in the final victory of the working people. From every corner we are receiving news that the masses are ready and willing to rise in the name of the Constituent Assembly. Don't be trapped into negotiations with the Bolsheviks. They will only enter into such negotiations in order to gain time and to concentrate around Kronstadt those formations of the privileged soviet military corps of which they can be sure. Glory to those who were the first to raise the flag of popular liberation. Down with the despotism of both right and left. Long live liberty and democracy.'

At the same time a second appeal was sent to Kronstadt by special courier, from the 'deputation abroad of the Socialist Revolutionary Party':

'The Party has abstained from any type of putchism. In Russia it has lately put the brakes on the upsurges of popular anger while frequently trying, through the pressure of worker and peasant opinion, to compel the Kremlin dictators to concede to the demands of the people. But now that popular anger has overflowed, now that the flag of popular revolution has been proudly hoisted over Kronstadt, our Party is offering the rebels the help of all the forces it can muster in the struggle for liberty and democracy. The SRs are prepared to share your fate and to win or die in your ranks. Let us know how we can help you. Long live the people's revolution. Long live free soviets and the Constituent Assembly!'

To these concrete proposals, Tchernov received, on March 3 1921, the following answer by radio:

'The Provisional Revolutionary Committee of the city of Kronstadt has received the greetings of comrade Tchernov, despatched from Reval. To all our brothers abroad we express our gratitude for their sympathy. We thank Comrade Tchernov for suggestions but ask him not to come for the time being until the matter has been clarified. For the time being we are noting his proposal.
Signed: Petrichenko President of the Provisional Revolutionary Committee.'

The Bolsheviks claim that the Provisional Revolutionary Committee consented in principle to Tchernov's arrival. They also claim that Tchernov made his offer to send provisions to

Kronstadt conditional on the rebels launching the slogan of the Constituent Assembly. On March 20, 1921 the communist Komarov declared at a meeting of the Petrograd Soviet that the Provisional Revolutionary Committee had asked Tchernov to wait for 12 days during which time the food situation in Kronstadt would have become such that it would be possible to launch the slogan asked for by the SRs. Komarov claimed that this information had been obtained in the course of the cross-questioning of Perepelkin a member of the Provisional Revolutionary Committee who had fallen into Bolshevik hands. Perepelkin was even alleged to have said that the President of the Provisional Revolutionary Committee had secretly sent a positive answer to Tchernov.

The sailor Perepelkin was shot and his 'confessions' cannot be verified. But in prison, just before, he had met the Menshevik Dan and had mentioned no such thing to him although during their joint exercise periods Perepelkin had provided Dan with many details concerning the insurrection. One is led to believe that already in 1921, Bolshevik 'justice' knew how to concoct confessions.

In an article published in January 1926, in *Znamia Borby*, organ of the left SRs, Petrichenko, President of the Provisional Revolutionary Committee, confirms the answer given to Tchernov by the committee. He explains that the Committee itself could not deal with this question. It proposed to hand the problem over to the newly elected soviet. Petrichenko adds 'I am describing things as they took place in reality and independent of my own political opinion'. As for Tchernov, he denies having posed conditions for the rebels. He claims openly to have supported the slogan of the Constituent Assembly, 'convinced that sooner or later the rebels would have adopted it'.

The Left SRs

In the June 1921 issue of their paper *Znamia* published abroad, this is how the left SRs outlined their programme:

'The essential aim of the left (internationalist) S.R. Party is the reconstitution of the soviets and the restoration of genuine Soviet power … We are aiming at the permanent re-establishment of the violated Constitution of the Soviet Republic, as adopted on June 10, 1918, at the Fifth All-Russian Congress of Soviets … the peasantry, which is the backbone of the working population in Russia, should have the right to dispose of its fate … another essential demand is the re-establishment of the self-activity and of the free initiative of the workers in the cities. Intensive labour cannot be demanded of men who are starving and half dead. First they must be fed and to this end it is essential to co-ordinate the interests of workers and peasants.'

The spirit of the '*Petropavlovsk*' Resolution is undoubtedly very close to that of the left S.R. programme. The left SRs, however, deny participation in the insurrection. In the same issue of *Znamia* one of their Moscow correspondents writes: 'At Kronstadt, there wasn't a single responsible representative of left populism. The whole movement developed without our participation. At the onset we were outside of it but it was nevertheless essentially left populist in outlook. Its slogans and its moral objectives are very close to our own'.

In the wish to establish historical truth we will now quote two further authorised testimonies, that of Lenin and that of the sailor Petrichenko, one of the leaders of the insurrection.

Lenin's Views

In his article 'The Tax in Kind'[7] this is what Lenin has to say about Kronstadt:

'In the spring of 1921, mainly as a result of the failure of the harvest and the dying of cattle, the condition of the peasantry, which was extremely bad already as a consequence of the war and blockade, became very much worse. This resulted in political vacillation which, generally speaking, expresses the very 'nature' of the small producer. The most striking expression of this vacillation was the Kronstadt mutiny There was very little of anything that was fully formed, clear and definite. We heard nebulous slogans about 'liberty', 'free trade', 'emancipation from serfdom', 'Soviets without the Bolsheviks', or new elections to the Soviets, or relief from 'party dictatorship', and so on and so forth. Both the Mensheviks and the Socialist-Revolutionaries declared the Kronstadt movement to be 'their own'.

Victor Chernov sent a runner to Kronstadt: on the proposal of this runner, the Menshevik Valk, one of the Kronstadt leaders, voted for the '*Constituent*.' In a flash, with radio-telegraphic speed, one might say, the White Guards mobilised all their forces '*for Kronstadt*'. The White Guard military experts in Kronstadt, a number of experts, and not Kozlovsky alone, drew up a plan for a landing of forces at Oranienbaum, a plan which

---

7   Ida Mett's quotations from Lenin are wrongly attributed to his article on 'The Tax in Kind'. This report was delivered at the 10th Party Congress, on March 15, 1921 (*Selected Works*, Volume 9, p. 107). In fact the quotations relate to an article on 'The Food Tax' (*Selected Works*, Volume 9, pp. 194-198). Ed. Solidarity.

frightened the vacillating Menshevik-Socialist-Revolutionary non-party masses.

More than fifty Russian White Guard newspapers published abroad are conducting a furious campaign 'for Kronstadt'. The big banks, all the forces of finance capital, are collecting funds to assist Kronstadt. The wise leader of the bourgeoisie and the landlords, the Cadet Milyukov, is patiently explaining to the fool Victor Chernov directly (and to Dan and Rozhkov who are in Petrograd jail for their connection with the Kronstadt Mensheviks, indirectly) that they need be in no hurry with their Constituent, and that they *can and must support the Soviets only without the Bolsheviks.*

Of course, it is easy to be cleverer than conceited fools like Chernov, the hero of petty-bourgeois phrases, or like Martov, the knight of philistine reformism painted to look like 'Marxism'. Properly speaking, the point is not that Milyukov, as an individual, is cleverer, but that because of his class position the party leader of the big bourgeoisie sees, understands the class essence and political interaction of things more clearly than the leaders of the petty bourgeoisie, the Chernovs and Martovs. The bourgeoisie is really a class force which inevitably rules under capitalism, both under a monarchy and in the most democratic republic, and which also inevitably enjoys the support of the world bourgeoisie.

But the petty bourgeoisie. i.e.. all the heroes of the Second International and of the 'Two-and-a-Half' International, cannot, by the very economic nature of the case, be anything else than the expression of class impotence; hence the vacillation, phrases and helplessness...

When in his Berlin Journal Martov declared that Kronstadt not only adopted Menshevik slogans but also proved that an anti-Bolshevik movement was possible which did not entirely serve the interests of the White Guards, the capitalists and the landlords, he served as an example of a conceited philistine Narcissus. He said in effect: 'Let us close our eyes to the fact that all the real White Guards greeted the Kronstadt mutineers and through the banks collected funds in aid of Kronstadt!' Kilyukov is right compared with the Chernovs and Martovs, for he proposes real tactics for a real White Guard Force, the force of the capitalists and landlords. He says in effect: 'It does not matter whom we support, even the anarchists, any sort of Soviet government, *as long as* the Bolsheviks are overthrown, *as long as shifting of power* can be brought about! It makes no difference, to the Right or to the Left, to the Mensheviks or to the anarchists, as long as power shifts away from the Bolsheviks.' As for the rest – 'we', the Milyukovs, we shall give the anarchists, the Chernovs and the Martovs a good slapping and kick them out as was done to Chernov and Maisky in Siberia, to the Hungarian Chernovs and Martovs in Hungary, to Kautsky in Germany and Friedrich Adler and Co. in Vienna. The real, practical bourgeoisie fooled hundreds of these philistine Narcissuses: the Mensheviks, Socialist-Revolutionaries and non-party people, and kicked them out scores of times in all revolutions in all countries. This is proved by history. It is corroborated by facts. The Narcissuses will chatter; the Milyukovs and White Guards will act...

The events of the spring of 1921 once again revealed the role of the Socialist-Revolutionaries and Mensheviks: they are helping the vacillating petty-bourgeois element to recoil from the Bolsheviks, to cause a 'shifting of power' for the benefit of the capitalists and landlords. The

Mensheviks and Socialist-Revolutionaries have now learnt to disguise themselves as 'non-party'.'

Petrichenko's Evidence

We will finally quote the main passages of Petrichenko's evidence, as published in his article in the left S.R. paper *Znamia Borby*, in January 1926:

'I have read the letters exchanged between the left S.R. organisation and the British Communists. In this correspondence the question of the Kronstadt insurrection of 1921 is raised...

As I was the President [of the Provisional Revolutionary Committee] I feel it a moral obligation briefly to throw some light on these events for the benefit of the Political Bureau of the British Communist Party. I know you get your information from Moscow. I also know that this information is one-sided and biased. It wouldn't be a bad thing if you were shown the other side of the coin....

You have yourselves admitted that the Kronstadt insurrection of 1921 was not inspired from the outside. This recognition implies that the patience of the working masses, sailors, red soldiers, workers and peasants had reached its final limit.

Popular anger against the dictatorship of the Communist Party – or rather against its bureaucracy – took the form of an insurrection. This is how precious blood came to be spilt. There was no question of class or caste differences. There were workers on both sides of the barricades. The difference lay in the fact that the men of Kronstadt marched forward consciously and of their own free will, while those who were attacking them had been misled by the Communist Party leaders and some were even acting against their own wishes. I can tell you even more: the Kronstadters didn't enjoy taking up arms and spilling blood!

What happened then to force the Kronstadters to speak the language of guns with the Communist Party bosses, daring to call themselves a 'Workers and Peasants Government'?

The Kronstadt sailors had taken an active part in the creation of such a government. They had protected it against all the attacks of the Counter-revolution. They not only protected the gates of Petrograd – the heart of the world revolution – but they also formed military detachments for the innumerable fronts against the White Guards, starting with Kornilov and finishing with Generals Youdienitch and Neklioudov.

You are asked to believe that these same Kronstadters had suddenly become the enemies of the Revolution. The 'Workers and Peasants' Government denounced the Kronstadt rebels as agents of the Entente, as French spies, as supporters of the bourgeoisie, as SRs, as Mensheviks, etc., etc. It is astounding that the men of Kronstadt should suddenly have become dangerous enemies just when real danger from the generals of the armed counter-revolution had disappeared – just when the rebuilding of the country had to be tackled – just when people were thinking of tasting the fruits of October – just when it was a question of showing the goods in their true colour, of showing one's political baggage (i.e. when it was no longer a question of making promises but of sticking to them). People were beginning to draw up a balance sheet of revolutionary achievements. We hadn't dared dream about this during the Civil War. Yet it is just at this point in time that the men of Kronstadt were found to be enemies. What crime had Kronstadt, there-fore, committed against the revolution?

As the Civil War subsided, the Petrograd workers thought it their right to remind the Soviet of that town that the time had come to remember their economic plight and to pass from a war regime to a regime of peace.

The Petrograd Soviet considered this harmless and essential demand to be counter-revolutionary. It not only remained deaf and dumb to these claims but it started resorting to home searches and arrests of workers, declaring them spies and agents of the Entente. These bureaucrats became corrupt during the Civil War at a time when no one dared resist them. They hadn't noticed that the situation had changed.

The workers answered by resorting to strikes. The fury of the Petrograd Soviet then became like the fury of a wild animal. Assisted by its Opritchniks[8] it kept the workers hungry and exhausted. It held them in an iron grip, driving them to work by all kinds of constraint. The Red soldiers and sailors, despite their sympathy with the workers, didn't dare rise in their defence. But this time the 'workers' and 'peasants' Government came unstuck about Kronstadt. Somewhat belatedly Kronstadt had learned about the true state of affairs in Petrograd.

You are therefore right, British comrades, when you say that the Kronstadt revolt was not the result of the activities of any one particular person.

---

8 The Opritchniks were the personal guard of Ivan the Terrible and at the same time his higher political police force. During the seven years of their existence (1565-1572) they distinguished themselves by their ferocious activity.

Furthermore I would like you to know more about the alleged support to Kronstadt of counter-revolutionary foreign and Russian organisations! I repeat again that the uprising was not provoked by any political organisation. I doubt they even existed at Kronstadt. The revolt broke out spontaneously. It expressed the wishes of the masses themselves, both the civilian population and the garrison. This is seen in the resolutions adopted and in the composition of the Provisional Revolutionary Committee, where one cannot detect the dominant influence of any anti-soviet party. According to the Kronstadters any thing that happened or was done there was dictated by the circumstances of the moment. The rebels didn't place their faith in anyone. They didn't even place it in the hands of the Provisional Revolutionary Committee or in the hands of the assemblies of delegates, or in the hands of meetings, or anywhere else. There was no question about this. The Provisional Revolutionary Committee never attempted anything in this direction, although it could have done. The Committee's only concern was strictly to implement the wishes of the people. Was that a good thing or a bad thing? I cannot pass judgement.

The truth is that the masses led the Committee and not the other way round. Among us there were no well-known political figures, of the kind who see everything three archines[9] deep and know all that needs to be done, and how to get the most out of every situation. The Kronstadters acted without predetermined plans or programme, feeling their way according to circumstances and within the context of the resolutions they had adopted. We were cut off from the entire world. We didn't

---

9 archine = Russian measure of length.

know what was going on outside Kronstadt, either in Russia or abroad. Some may possibly have drawn up their own blueprints for our insurrection as usually happens. They were wasting their time. It is fruitless to speculate as to what would have happened if things had evolved differently, for the turn of events itself might have been quite different from what we were anticipating. One thing is certain, the Kronstadters didn't want the initiative to pass out of their hands.

In their publications the Communists accuse us of accepting an offer of food and medicine from the Russian Red Cross, in Finland. We admit we saw nothing wrong in accepting such an offer. Both the Provisional Revolutionary Committee and the assembly of delegates agreed to it. We felt that the Red Cross was a philanthropic organisation, offering us disinterested help that could do us no harm. When we decided to allow the Red Cross delegation to enter Kronstadt we lead them blindfolded to our head-quarters. At our first meeting we informed them that we gratefully accepted their offer of help as coming from a philanthropic organisation, but that we considered ourselves free of any undertakings towards them. We accepted their request to leave a permanent representative in Kronstadt, to watch over the regular distribution to women and children of the rations which they were proposing to send us.

Their representative, a retired naval officer called Vilken, remained in Kronstadt. He was put in a permanently guarded flat and couldn't even step outside without our permission. What danger could this man have represented? All he could see was the resolve of the garrison and of the civilian population of Kronstadt.

Was this the 'aid of the international bourgeoisie'? Or did this aid perhaps lie in the fact that Victor Tchernov had sent us his greetings? Was this the 'support of both the Russian and international counter-revolution'? Can you really believe that the men of Kronstadt were ready to throw themselves into the embrace of any anti-soviet party? Remember that when the rebels learned that the right wing was beginning to devise plans about their insurrection they didn't hesitate to warn the workers about it. Remember the article of March 6 in the Kron-stadt *Izvestia*, entitled 'gentlemen or comrades'.'

Kronstadt: Last Upsurge of the Soviets

'... this luxury was really absolutely impermissible. By permitting (sic!) such a discussion (on the trade unions) we undoubtedly made a mistake and failed to see that in this discussion a question came to the forefront which, because of the objective conditions, should not have been in the forefront ...' Lenin. Report to 10th Party Congress, March 8, 1921. *Selected Works*, Vol. IX, p. 90.

'What the rebels of Kronstadt demanded was only what Trotsky had promised their elder brothers and what he and the Party had been unable to give. Once again a bitter and hostile echo of his own voice came back to him from the lips of other people, and once again he had to suppress it.' Isaac Deutscher, *The Prophet Armed*, p. 512-3

Trotsky's Accusations

Taking everything into account, what was the Kronstadt uprising? Was it a counter-revolutionary insurrection? Was it a revolt without conscious counter-revolutionary objectives, but which was bound to open the doors to the counter-revolution? Or was it simply an attempt by the working masses to materialise some of the promise of October? Was the revolt inevitable? And was the bloody end to which it came also inevitable? We will conclude by trying to answer these questions.

The accusations made against Kronstadt by the Bolsheviks in 1921 are exactly the same as those mentioned later by the Stalinist historian Poukhov, in his book published in 1931. Trotsky repeated them. The trotskyists still repeat them today.

Trotsky's attitude on this question was however always somewhat embarrassed and awkward. He would issue his accusations by the dropper instead of proclaiming them once and for all. In 1937, when he discussed Kronstadt for the first time in writing (in his books on the Russian Revolution he hardly ever dealt with the subject) he starts by saying that 'The country was hungry, and the Kronstadt sailors were demanding privileges. The mutiny was motivated by their wish for privileged rations.'[1] Such a demand was never put forward by the men of Kronstadt. In his later writings Trotsky, having doubtless taken care to read more on the matter, was to abandon this particular accusation. What remains, however, is that he started his public accusations with a lie.

In an article in the Belgian paper *Lutte Ouvriére* (February 26, 1938) Trotsky wrote:

'From a class point of view, which – no offence to the eclectics – remains the fundamental criterion both in

---

1 Bulletin of the Opposition, No. 56-57 (In Russian).

politics and in history, it is extremely important to compare the conduct of Kronstadt with that of Petrograd during these critical days. In Petrograd too the whole leading stratum of the working class had been skimmed off. Famine and cold reigned in the abandoned capital, even more cruelly than in Moscow... The paper of the Kronstadt rebels spoke of barricades in Petrograd, of thousands of people killed.[2] The Press of the whole world was announcing the same thing. In fact the exact opposite took place. The Kronstadt uprising did not attract the workers of Petrograd. It repelled them. The demarcation took place along class lines. The workers immediately felt that the Kronstadt rebels were on the other side of the barricade and they gave their support to the Government.'

Here again Trotsky is saying things which are quite untrue. Earlier on we showed how the wave of strikes had started in Petrograd and how Kronstadt had followed suit. It was against the strikers of Petrograd that the Government had to organise a special General Staff: the Committee of Defence. The repression was first directed against the Petrograd workers and against their demonstrations, by the despatch of armed detachments of Koursantys.[3]

But the workers of Petrograd had no weapons. They could not defend themselves as could the Kronstadt sailors. The military repression directed against Kronstadt certainly intimidated the Petrograd workers. The demarcation did not take place 'along class lines' but according to the respective strengths of the organs of repression. The fact that the workers

---

2   It is untrue that the paper of the Kronstadters, the *Kronstadt Izvestia* ever spoke of 'thousands of people killed' in Petrograd.

3   Officer cadets.

of Petrograd did not follow those of Kronstadt does not prove that they did not sympathise with them. Nor, at a later date, when the Russian proletariat failed to follow the various 'oppositions' did this prove that they were in agreement with Stalin! In such instances it was a question of the respective strengths of the forces confronting one another.

In the same article Trotsky repeats his points concerning the exhaustion of Kronstadt, from the revolutionary point of view. He claims that, whereas the Kronstadt sailors of 1917 and 1918 were ideologically at a much higher level than the Red Army, the contrary was the case by 1921. This argument is refuted by official Red Army documents. These admit that the frame of mind of Kronstadt had infected large layers of the army.

Trotsky denounces those who attack him over Kronstadt over the belatedness of their strictures. 'The campaign around Kronstadt' he says 'is conducted, in certain places, with unrelenting energy. One might imagine that events took place yesterday and not seventeen years ago!' But seventeen years is a very short period, on any historical scale. We don't accept that to speak of Kronstadt is to 'evoke the days of the Egyptian Pharaohs'. Moreover it appears logical to us to seek some of the roots of the great Russian catastrophe in this striking and symptomatic episode. After all it took place at a time when the repression of the Russian workers was not being perpetrated by some Stalin or other but by the flower of Bolshevism, by Lenin and Trotsky themselves. Seriously to discuss the Kronstadt revolt is therefore not, as Trotsky claims, 'to be interested in discrediting the only genuinely revolutionary tendency, the only tendency never to have reneged its flag, never to have compromised with the enemy, the only tendency to represent the future'.

During the subsequent seventeen years Trotsky shed none of his hostility towards the rebels. Lacking arguments he resorts to gossip. He tells us that 'at Kronstadt, where the garrison was doing nothing and only living on its past, demoralisation had reached important proportions. When the situation became particularly difficult in famished Petrograd, the Political Bureau discussed several times whether to raise an internal loan in Kronstadt, where there still remained old stores of all SRs. But the Petrograd delegates would answer: 'They will give us nothing of their own free will. They speculate on cloth, coal, bread, for in Kronstadt all the old scum has raised its head again!'.

This argument concerning 'old stores of all SRs' is in bad faith. One need only recall the ultimatum to the Kronstadters issued by the Petrograd Defence Committee on March 5th (referred to elsewhere): 'You will be obliged to surrender. Kronstadt has neither bread nor fuel'. What had happened in the meantime to the said old stories

Further information on this topic comes from the *Kronstadt Izvestia*. It describes the distribution to children of one pound of dried potatoes on presentation of ration vouchers 5 and 6. On March 8th, four litres of oats were distributed to last four days – and on March 9th a quarter of a pound of black biscuit made of flour and dried potato powder. On March 10th the Regional Committee of Metalworkers decided to place at the disposal of the community the horse meat to which its members were entitled. During the insurrection there was also distributed a tin of condensed milk per person, on one occasion some meat preserves, and finally (to children only), half a pound of butter.

That no doubt is what Trotsky refers to as 'old stores of all SRs'! According to him these might have been borrowed to alleviate the great Russian famine. We should add that before the insurrection these 'stores' were in the hands of communist functionaries and that it was upon these people alone that consent to the proposed 'loan' depended. The rank and file sailor, who took part in the insurrection, had no means open to him whereby he could have opposed the loan, even if he had wanted to. So much for the question of 'stores' – which in passing shows the worth of some of the accusations used against Kronstadt.

To resort to such arguments in the course of a serious discussion (and consciously to substitute for such a discussion a polemic about the Spanish Revolution) shows up a serious flaw: the absence of valid arguments on the matter among the Bolsheviks (for Trotsky isn't the central figure in the repression of Kronstadt. Lenin and the Politbureau directed the whole operation. The Workers' Opposition must also shoulder its share of responsibility. According to the personal testimony of foreign Communists residing in Russia at the time, the Workers' Opposition didn't agree with the measures being taken against the rebels. But neither did it dare open its mouth for the defence of Kronstadt. At the 10th Party Congress no one protested at the butchery of the rebels. The worker Lutovinov, a well known member of the Central Executive Committee of the Soviets and one of the leaders of the Workers Opposition, was sent to Berlin in March 1921 on a diplomatic mission (in reality this was a form of political exile). He declared that: 'The news published abroad concerning the Kronstadt events was greatly exaggerated. The Soviet Government is strong enough to finish off the rebels. The slowness of the operation is to be explained by the fact that we wish to spare the population of Kronstadt'. ('*L'Humanite*'. March 18, 1921)[4]

---

4   Lutovinov committed suicide in Moscow, in May 1924.

Trotsky uses yet another argument against the rebels: he accuses them of seeking to take advantage of their revolutionary past. This is a most dangerous argument for anyone in opposition. Stalin was to use it against Trotsky and the old Bolsheviks. It was only later that Stalin accused them of having been, from the very beginning of the Revolution, the agents of the international bourgeoisie. During the first years of the struggle he conceded that Trotsky had rendered great services to the Revolution but he would add that Trotsky had subsequently passed into the ranks of the counter-revolution. One had to judge a man on what he did now. The example of Mussolini was constantly mentioned.

However, there are many things that Trotsky is unable to explain. He cannot explain how Kronstadt and the whole Red Fleet came to renounce their ideological support for the Government. He cannot explain the frame of mind of the communist elements in the Fleet during the discussions on the Trade Union question. He cannot explain their attitude during the 8th All-Russian Soviet Congress elections or during the Second Communist Conference of the Baltic Fleet, which took place on the eve of the insurrection. These are, however, key points around which the discussion should centre. When Trotsky asserts that all those supporting the government were genuinely proletarian and progressive, whereas all others represented the peasant counter-revolution, we have a right to ask of him that he present us with a serious factual analysis in support of his contention. The unfurling of subsequent events showed that the Revolution was being shunted onto a disastrously wrong track. This was first to compromise then to destroy all its social, political, and moral conquests. Did the Kronstadt revolt really represent an attempt to guide the Revolution along new lines? That is the crucial question one has to ask. Other problems should be seen as of secondary importance and flowing from this serious concern.

It is certainly not the smashing of the Kronstadt revolt that put a brake to the course of the Revolution. On the contrary, in our opinion, it was the political methods used against Kronstadt and widely practised throughout Russia which contributed to the setting up, on the ruins of the Social Revolution, of an oligarchic regime which had nothing in common with the original ideas of the Revolution.[5]

The Bolshevik Interpretations

In 1921 the Bolshevik Government claimed that Kronstadt had rebelled according to a preconceived plan. This particular interpretation was based on a note published in certain French newspapers (*Le Matin*, *L'Echo de Paris*) on February 15th. This note announced the uprising and led to the claim that the uprising was led by the Entente.

This was the argument which enabled Lenin to claim, at the 10th Party Congress:

---

5   In his last book, written in the tragic context of an unequal struggle with his mortal enemy, Trotsky made what was for him a great effort at being objective. This is what he says about Kronstadt: 'The Stalinist school of falsification is not the only one that flourishes today in the field of Russian history. Indeed, it derives a measure of sustenance from certain legends built on ignorance and sentimentalism, such as the lurid tales concerning Kronstadt, Makhno and other episodes of the Revolution. Suffice it to say that what the Soviet Government did reluctantly at Kronstadt was a tragic necessity; naturally the revolutionary government could not have 'presented' the fortress that protected Petrograd to the insurgent sailors only because a few dubious Anarchists and SRs were sponsoring a handful of reactionary peasants and soldiers in rebellion. Similar considerations were involved in the case of Makhno and other potentially revolutionary elements that were perhaps well-meaning but definitely ill-acting.' *Stalin* by Trotsky. Hollis and Carter (1947), p. 337.

'The transfer of political power from the hands of the Bolsheviks to a vague conglomeration or alliance of het-erogeneous elements who seem to be only a little to the Right of the Bolsheviks, and perhaps even to the 'Left' of the Bolsheviks – so indefinite is the sum of political groupings which tried to seize power in Kronstadt. Undoubtedly, at the same time, White generals – you all know it – played a great part in this. This is fully proved. The Paris newspapers reported a mutiny in Kronstadt two weeks before the events in Kronstadt took place.'[6]

The publication of false news about Russia was nothing excep-tional. Such news was published before, during, and after the Kronstadt events. It is undeniable that the bourgeoisie throughout the world was hostile to the Russian Revolution and would exaggerate any bad news emanating from that country. The Second Communist Conference of the Baltic Fleet had just voted a resounding resolution, critical of the political leadership of the Fleet. This fact could easily have been exaggerated by the bourgeois press, once again confusing the wishes with reality. To base an accusation on a 'proof' of this kind is inadmissible and immoral.

In 1938 Trotsky himself was to drop this accusation. But in the article we have already mentioned he refers his readers to a study of the Kronstadt rebellion undertaken by an American trotskyst John G Wright. In an article published in the *New International* (in February 1938) Mr Wright takes up once again the claim that the revolt must have been planned before-hand. In view of the fact the press had announced it on February 15th. He says: 'the connection between Kronstadt and the counter-revolution can be established not only out of the mouths of the enemies of Bolshevism but also on the basis

---

6   Lenin. *Selected Works*. Lawrence and Wishart (1937). Volume 9, p. 97.

of irrefutable facts'. What irrefutable facts? Again, quotations from the bourgeois press (*Le Matin*, *Vossische Zeitung*, *The Times*) giving false news before and during the insurrection.

It is interesting that these arguments were not much used at the time, during the battle itself, but only years later. If, at the time the Bolshevik Government had proofs of these alleged contacts between Kronstadt and the counter-revolutionaries why did it not try the rebels publicly? Why did it not show the working masses of Russia the 'real' reasons for the uprising? If this wasn't done it was because no such proofs existed.

We are also told that if the New Economic policy had been introduced in time the insurrection would have been avoided. But as we have just shown the uprising did not take place according to a preconceived plan. No one knew that it was necessarily going to take place. We have no theory as to the exact timing and development of popular movements and it is quite possible that under economic and political conditions different from those prevailing in the spring of 1921 the insurrection might never have taken place. On the other hand the uprising might have occurred in a different form, or in a different place, for instance in Nijni Novgorod where an important strike movement took place, coinciding with the great strike wave in Petrograd. The particular conditions relating to the Fleet and to Kronstadt's revolutionary past certainly had an effect, but one can't be certain just exactly how significant this effect was. Much the same applies to the statement that 'if the N.E.P. had been introduced a few months earlier there would have been no Kronstadt revolt'.

The N.E P. was admittedly proclaimed at the same time as the rebels were being massacred. But it doesn't follow in any way that the N.E.P. corresponded to the demands put forward by the sailors. In the Kronstadt *Izvestia* of March 14th we find a characteristic passage on this subject. The rebels proclaimed that 'Kronstadt is not asking for freedom of trade but for genuine power to the Soviets'. The Petrograd strikers were also demanding the reopening of the markets and the abolition of the road blocks set up by the militia. But they too were stating that freedom of trade by itself would not solve their problems.

Insofar as the N.E.P. replaced the forced requisition of foodstuffs by the tax in kind and insofar as it re-established internal trade it certainly satisfied some of the demands of the men of Kronstadt and of the striking Petrograd workers. With the N.E.P. rationing and arbitrary seizures ceased. Petty owners were able to sell their goods on the open markets, lessening the effects on the great famine. The N.E.P. appeared to be first and foremost a safety measure.

But the N.E.P. unleashed the capitalist elements in the country just at a time when the one party dictatorship was leaving the proletariat and working peasants without means of defence against these capitalist forces. 'The class exerting the dictatorship is in fact deprived of the most elementary political rights' proclaimed the Worker's Truth, an oppositional communist group in 1922. The Worker's Group, another oppositional tendency, characterised the situation as follows: 'The working class is totally deprived of rights, the trade unions being a blind instrument in the hands of the function-aries'.

This was certainly not what the Kronstadt rebels were asking for! On the contrary. They were proposing measures which would have restored to the working class and working peasantry their true place in the new regime. The Bolsheviks only implemented the least important demands of the Kron-stadt programme (those coming in eleventh place in the resolution of the rebels!). They totally ignored the basic demand, the demand for workers' democracy!

The Kronstadt Uprising

This demand, put forward in the Petropavlovsky resolution was neither utopian nor dangerous. We here take issue with Victor Serge. In *Revolution Proletarienne* (of September 10th, 1937) Serge stated that 'while the sailors were engaged in mortal combat, they put forward a demand which, at that particular moment, was extremely dangerous – although quite genuine and sincerely revolutionary: the demand for freely elected soviets... they wished to unleash a cleansing tornado but in practice they could only have opened the doors to the peasant counter-revolution, of which the Whites and foreign intervention would have taken advantage... Insurgent Kronstadt was not counter-revolutionary, but its victory would inevitably have led to the counter-revolution.' Contrary to Serge's assertion we believe that the political demands of the sailors were full of a deep political wisdom. They were not derived from any abstract theory but from a profound awareness of the conditions of Russian life. They were in no way counter-revolutionary.

Rosa Luxemburg's Views

It is worth recalling what Rosa Luxemburg, a political personality respected throughout the world as a great socialist militant, had written about the lack of democracy in the leadership of the Russian Revolution, as early as 1918.

'It is an incontestable fact', she wrote, 'that the rule of the broad, popular masses is inconceivable without unlimited freedom of the press, without absolute freedom of meeting and of association... the gigantic tasks which the Bolsheviks have tackled with courage and resolution require the most intensive political education of the masses and accumulation of experience which is impossible without political freedom. Freedom restricted to those who support the Government or to Party members only, however numerous they may be, is not real freedom. Freedom is always freedom for the one who thinks differently. This is not because of fanaticism for abstract justice but because everything that is instructive, healthy and cleansing in political liberty hinges on this and because political liberty loses its value when freedom becomes a privilege.'

'We have never worshipped at the altar of formal democracy,' she continued. 'We have always distinguished between the social content and the political form of bourgeois democracy. The historical task facing the proletariat after its accession to power is to replace bourgeois democracy by proletarian democracy, not to abolish all democracy... The dictatorship (of the proletariat) consists in the way democracy is applied, not in its abolition. It must be the action of the class and not of a small minority, managing things in the name of the class.... If political life throughout the country is stifled it must fatally follow that life in the soviets themselves will be paralysed. Without general elections, without unlimited freedom of the press and of assembly, without free confrontation of opinions, life will dry up in all public institutions – or it will be only a sham life, where the bureaucracy is the only active element.'

We have dwelt on these quotations to show that Rosa Luxembourg, in her statements about the need for democracy, went much further than the Kronstadt rebels. They restricted their comments about democracy to matters of interest to the proletariat and to the working peasantry. Moreover Rosa Luxemburg formulated her criticisms of the Russian Revolution in 1918, in a period of full civil war, whereas the Petropavlovsk resolution was voted at a time when the armed struggle had virtually come to an end.

Would anyone dare accuse Rosa, on the basis of her criticisms, of having been in collusion with the international bourgeoisie? Why then are the demands of the Kronstadt sailors denounced as 'dangerous' and as inevitably leading to the counter-revolution? Has not the subsequent evolution of events amply vindicated both the Kronstadt rebels and Rosa Luxemburg? Was Rosa Luxemburg not right when she asserted that the task of the working class was to exercise working class power and not the dictatorship of a party or of a clique? For Rosa Luxemburg working class power was defined as 'the achievement in a contest of the widest discussion, of the most active and unlimited participation of the popular masses in an unrestricted democracy.'

A Third Soviet Revolution

When putting forward their democratic demands, the Kronstadt rebels had probably never heard of the writings of Rosa Luxemburg. What they had heard of, however, was the first Constitution of the Soviet Republic, voted on July 10, 1918, by the 5th All Russian Congress of Soviets. Articles 13, 14, 15 and 16 of the Constitution assured all workers of certain democratic rights (freedom of worship, freedom of assembly, freedom of union, freedom of the press). These articles sought to prevent the allocation of special privileges to any specific group or Party (articles 22 and 23).

The same Constitution proclaimed that no worker could be deprived of the right to vote or of the right to stand as a candidate, provided he satisfied the conditions stipulated in articles 64 and 65, that is to say provided he did not exploit the labour of others or live off income other than that which he had earned.

The central demand of the Kronstadt insurrection – all power to the Soviets (and not to the Party) – was in fact based on an article of the Constitution. This proclaimed that all central and local power would henceforth be precisely in the hands of the soviets!

From the very beginning this Constitution was violated by the Bolsheviks – or rather its provisions were never put into effect. It is worth recalling that Rosa Luxemburg's criticisms were formulated a few months after the vote of this new constitution charter. When in 1921 the sailors were to insist on a genuine application of the rights they had acquired in 1918 they were called 'counter-revolutionaries' and denounced as 'agents of the international bourgeoisie'. Sixteen years later Victor Serge was to say that the demands of the rebels would necessarily have led to the counter-revolution. This shows how deep-going were Bolshevik attitudes concerning the dangers of democracy.

The basic laws of the Soviet Republic constitute a juridical summary of the ideology of the October Revolution. By the end of the Civil War these ideas had been pushed so far back that a third revolution would have been necessary to reinstate them and have them applied in everyday life. This is what the Kronstadt rebels meant when they spoke of the Third Revolution. In the Kronstadt *Izvestia* of March 8 they wrote: 'At Kronstadt the foundation stone has been laid of the Third Revolution. This will break the final chains which still bind the working masses and wall open up new paths of socialist creation'.

We do not know if it would have been possible to save the conquests of October by democratic methods. We do not know if the economic situation of the country and its markedly peasant character were really suitable for the first attempt at building socialism. These problems should be discussed. But the task of those seeking truth is to proclaim the facts without embellishments. It is not good enough to take a superciliously scientific air to explain away historical phenomena.

When Trotsky sought to explain the development of the bureaucracy which had strangled all real life in the institutions of the Soviet State he found no difficulty in outlining his conception. In *The Revolution Betrayed* he states that one of the important causes was the fact that demobilised Red Army officers had come to occupy leading positions in the local soviets and had introduced military methods into them – at a time when the proletariat was exhausted following the prolonged revolutionary upheaval. This apparently led to the birth of the bureaucracy. Trotsky omits to recall how he himself sought to introduce precisely these methods into the trade unions. Was it to save the proletariat further fatigue? And if the proletariat was that exhausted how come it was still capable of waging virtually total general strikes in the largest and most heavily industrialised cities? And if the Party was still really the driving force of the social revolution how come it did not help the proletariat in the struggle against the nascent, but already powerful, bureaucracy – instead of shooting the workers down, at a time when their energy had been sapped by three years of imperialist war followed by three years of civil war.

Why did the Communist Party identify itself with the authoritarian state? The answer is that the Party was no longer revolutionary. It was no longer proletarian. And this is precisely what the men of Kronstadt were blaming the Party for. Their merit is to have said all this in 1921 – when it might still have been possible to change the situation – and not to have waited 15 years, by which time the defeat had become irrevocable.

Bureaucracy is almost a hereditary hallmark in Russia. It is as old as the Russian state itself. The Bolsheviks in power not only inherited the Tsarist bureaucracy itself, but its very spirit. Its very atmosphere. They should have realised that as the state enlarged its functions to encompass economic affairs, as it became the owner of all natural wealth and of industry, an immediate danger would arise of the rebirth and rapid development of the bureaucratic frame of mind.

A doctor treating a patient with a bad heredity takes this into account and advises certain precautions. What precautions did the Bolsheviks take to combat the bureaucratic tendencies which were obvious, in the very first years of the Revolution? What methods could they have used other than to allow a powerful democratic draught to blow through the whole atmosphere, and to encourage a rigorous and effective control to be exerted by the working masses?

True enough, some form of control was envisaged. The trouble was that the Commissariat of the Workers and Peasants inspection was to entrust this control to the very same type of bureaucrat whose power it was seeking to thwart. One need not seek far to find the causes of the bureaucratisation. Its roots lay deeply in the Bolshevik concept of the State commanded and controlled by a single Party, itself organised along absolutist and bureaucratic lines. These causes were of course aggravated by Russia's own bureaucratic traditions.

It is wrong to blame the peasantry for the defeat of the Revolution and for its degeneration into a bureaucratic regime. It would be too easy to explain all Russia's difficulties by the agrarian character of her economy. Some people seem to say at one and the same time that the Kronstadt revolt against the bureaucracy was a peasant revolt and that the bureaucracy itself was of peasant origin. With such a concept of the role of the peasantry one may ask how the Bolsheviks dared advocate the idea of the socialist revolution? How did they dare struggle for it in an agrarian country?

Some claim that the Bolsheviks allowed themselves such actions (as the suppression of Kronstadt) in the hope of a forthcoming world revolution, of which they considered themselves the vanguard. But would not a revolution in another country have been influenced by the spirit of the Russian Revolution? When one considers the enormous moral authority of the Russian Revolution throughout the world one may ask oneself whether the deviations of this Revolution would not eventually have left an imprint on other countries. Many historical facts allow such a judgement. One may recognise the impossibility of genuine socialist construction in a single country, yet have doubts as to whether the bureaucratic deformations of the Bolshevik regime would have been straightened out by the winds coming from revolutions in other countries.

The fascist experience in countries like Germany shows that an advanced stage of capitalist development is an insufficient guarantee against the growth of absolutist and autocratic tendencies. Although this is not the place to explain the phenomenon, we must note the powerful wave of authoritarianism coming from economically advanced countries and threatening to engulf old ideas and traditions. It is incontestable that Bolshevism is morally related to this absolutist frame of mind. It had in fact set a precedent for subsequent tendencies. No one can be sure that had another revolution occurred elsewhere following the one in Russia, Bolshevism would have democratised itself. It might again have revealed its absolutist features.

Were there not real dangers in the democratic way? Was there no reason to fear reformist influences in the soviets, if democracy had been given free rein? We accept that this was a real danger. But it was no more of a danger than what inevitably followed the uncontrolled dictatorship of a single party, whose General Secretary was already Stalin.[7]

We are told that the country was at the end of its tether, that it had lost its ability to resist. True, the country was weary of war. But on the other hand it was full of constructive forces, ardently seeking to learn and to educate themselves. The end of the Civil War saw a surge of workers and peasants towards schools, workers' universities and institutes of technical education. Wasn't this yearning the best testimony to the vitality and resistance of these classes? In a country with a very high level of illiteracy, such an education could greatly have helped the working masses in the genuine exercise of real power.

But by its very essence a dictatorship destroys the creative capacities of a people. Despite the undoubted attempts of the Government to educate workers, education soon became the privilege of Party members loyal to the leading faction. From 1921 on, workers' faculties and higher educational establishments were purged of their more independent minded elements. This process gained tempo with the development of oppositional tendencies within the Party. The attempt at a genuine mass education was increasingly compromised. Lenin's wish that every cook should be able to govern the state became less and less likely to be implemented.

The revolutionary conquest could only be deepened through a genuine participation of the masses. Any attempt to substitute an 'elite' for those masses could only be profoundly reactionary.

In 1921 the Russian Revolution stood at the cross roads. The democratic or the dictatorial way, that was the question. By

---

7 Ida Matt is wrong in implying that Stalin was General Secretary of the Party at the time of the events she is describing. The post of General Secretary – and Stalin's appointment to it (incidentally endorsed by both Lenin and Trotsky) – only took place in 1922. (Ed. Solidarity).

lumping together bourgeois and proletarian democracy the Bolsheviks were in fact condemning both. They sought to build socialism from above, through skilful manoeuvres of the Revolutionary General Staff. While waiting for a world revolution that was not round the corner, they built a state capitalist society, where the working class no longer had the right to make the decisions most intimately concerning it.

Lenin was not alone in perceiving that the Kronstadt rebellion was a challenge to this plan. Both he and the Bolsheviks were fully aware that what was at stake was the monopoly of their Party. Kronstadt might have opened the way to a genuine proletarian democracy, incompatible with the Party's monopoly of power. That is why Lenin preferred to destroy Kronstadt. He chose an ignoble but sure way: the calumny that Kronstadt was allied to the bourgeoisie and to the agrarian counter-revolution.

When Kouzmin, Commissar to the Baltic Fleet, had stated at the Kronstadt meeting of March 2nd that the Bolsheviks would not surrender power without a fight, he was saying the truth. Lenin must have laughed at this Commissar who obviously didn't understand the ABC of Bolshevik morality or tactics. Politically and morally one had to destroy the opponent – not argue with him using real arguments. And destroy its revolutionary opponents is exactly what the Bolshevik government did.

The Kronstadt rebels were a grey, amorphous mass. But such masses occasionally show an incredible level of political awareness. If there had been among them a number of men of 'higher' political understanding the insurrection might well never have taken place, for those men would have understood firstly that the demands of the rebels were in flagrant conflict with the policies of the Kremlin – and secondly that, at that particular moment in time, the government felt itself firmly enough in the saddle to shoot down, without pity or mercy, any tendency daring seriously to oppose its views or plans.

The men of Kronstadt were sincere but naive. Believing in the justness of their cause they did not foresee the tactics of their opponents. They waited for help from the rest of the country, whose demands they knew they were voicing. They lost sight of the fact that the rest of the country was already in the iron grip of a dictatorship which no longer allowed the people the free expression of its wishes and the free choice of its institutions.

The great ideological and political discussion between 'realists' and 'dreamers' between 'scientific socialists' and the 'revolutionary volnitza'[8] was fought out, weapons in hand. It ended, in 1921, with the political and military defeat of the 'dreamers'. But Stalin was to prove to the whole world that this defeat was also the defeat of socialism, over a sixth of the earth's surface.

---

8   'open conference'.

Theory and Practice Publications

The Alternative to Capitalism – Adam Buick & John Crump

"Many books on capitalism document its mechanisms and effects without offering a positive outlook. This documentation, although vital, does not help us build the forward thinking needed to inspire a generation that change is possible, which is key if environmental catastrophe and other crises are to be halted. Buick and Crump's work is different – it defies the adage that it is easier to imagine the end of the world than the end of capitalism, taking a more progress-oriented outlook." Laura Potts – The Norwich Radical

The Joy of Revolution – Ken Knabb

"The Joy of Revolution, is a simple, but not simplistic, outline of why and how a non-hierarchical, non-statist society might be possible... I'd especially recommend the book for people who are vaguely sympathetic to the idea of a non-hierarchical, non-statist society but who are skeptical of how, in practice, it could ever happen. There are some pointers given and some common bugbears demolished along the way. And it is all written with that rare combination of readability and logicality and elan." Eugenia Lovelace – Red and Black

With the Peasants of Aragon – Augustin Souchy

In 1936, the people of Spain rose up, overthrew their masters and took power into their own hands. In the villages and small towns of Aragon, they began to live in a way never seen before in modern Europe. Their ideal – libertarian communism.

Available from Active Distribution, AK Press and all good booksellers